ABSA

PILANESBERG

CREATED BY JACANA

DISCOVER THE MAGIC

Jacana

ABSA GROUP

As the largest banking group of its kind in Africa, the ABSA Group is proud to be associated with an interpretative eco-series on top holiday destinations in South Africa. ABSA Group's commitment to South Africa, its people and its future is indelibly woven into its purpose and mission statement "to be partners in growing South Africa's prosperity, by being the leading financial services group serving all our stakeholders." By harnessing the rich diversity of this country's talent, both within and outside the Group, ABSA is confident it will achieve this.

The Group plays a significant role in the economic and social fabric of South Africa. ABSA Bank's extensive retail banking network throughout South Africa, comprising branches and agencies of Allied Bank, TrustBank, United Bank, and Volkskas Bank, offers a full range of personal and commercial banking services. The Group has 37 800 staff members and serves a diverse base of some 6 million customers.

Through the ABSA Foundation, the Group runs community development programmes at national and provincial level, and is an enthusiastic supporter of programmes designed to uplift the nation. ABSA Bank is also the leading provider of affordable home finance to the underprivileged.

This publication takes a closer look at the Pilanesberg. The Reserve offers a unique wildlife experience, as well as a journey through one of the most fascinating natural history areas in South Africa. Pilanesberg falls within the North West Province where the ABSA Group sponsors many community upliftment projects. Most of these are concentrated in the field of education. Through these projects, the ABSA Group strives to grow and prosper with the people of South Africa.

The North West is rich in art and culture and boasts a very unique human history. This publication brings all the magic of the Pilanesberg to life. We hope that you enjoy your travels and drive safely.

ABSA GROUP

Philip Hendrickse – ABSA Group

Acknowledgements

North West Parks
Steve Johnson, Hector Magome, Johnson Maoka, Koos Herbst, Bruce Brocket, Phil Johnson, Lowain Van Velden, Gus van Dyke, Les Ashley, Greg Stuart-Hill, Moses Mothusi, Bernard Marobe, Wilf Slade, Doc Shongwe

Goldfields Education Centre
Matlhomola Molwantwa, Billy Leketi, Rapula Ratsoga, Kenny Ditsi, Mac Magodielo, Moremi Lesejane, Moses Thebe

Text Development
Keryn Adcock,
Dave Gear (Saint Stithian's College),
Dr. John Bristow
(Minerals and Energy Policy Centre),
Professor Grant Cawthorn
(Wits Geological Dept),
Simon Hall (Wits Archaeology Dept),
Francois Coetzee (UNISA Archaeology Dept),
Ria Milburn (Bush Education Safaris)

Design
Original design: VIVO Design Associates
Re-design: Lisl Barry

Artists
Glynis Clouston, Sally MacLarty, Joan van Gogh, Melanie Wes, Mike Parkin

Photography
Paul Funston, Gus van Dyk, Gary van der Merwe

Translations
Ephraim Morei, T J Matebesi

Desk Top Publishing
Jacana Education, Anne Centner (Concept Training), Claire Waters, Belinda Bompani, Lana du Croq

Glossary

aphid – a tiny insect (bug) that lives on plants, causing them harm

aphrodisiac – a substance that arouses sexual desire

aquatic – an animal or plant that lives in water

arid – an area of insufficient water to support lush vegetation

bachelor herd – a herd of male antelope that do not hold a breeding herd territory of their own

barometer – an instrument that measures atmospheric pressure

bosses – the hard projection on the front of the head or horns of some animals

breeding herd – a herd of female antelope in season, kept together by a dominant male that mates with each female

browser – an animal that mainly eats leaves

camouflage – a method of disguising or concealing animals by their colouring

carcass – the dead body of an animal

carnivorous/carnivore – an animal that eats meat

carrion – the meat of a dead animal (sometimes rotten)

carrying capacity – the maximum number of animals an area can hold without causing damage to that area

catchment area – an area from which rain drains into a river or dam

census – an official count of the animal population

cere – the bare coloured skin at the base of bill of a bird of prey

chiefdoms – an area controlled by one chief

circumcision – cutting off the foreskin of a male person, usually as a religious practice

colony – birds that breed together in large groups

conserving – keeping from harm or loss, for future use

contour drain – a man-made furrow which channels water and helps prevent soil wash away

courtship display – the behaviour shown by animals while trying to attract their sexual partners

crust – the rocky outer layer of the earth's surface

crustacean – an animal that has a hard shell

cytotoxin – a poison that destroys the body's tissue

deciduous – a plant that loses its leaves during winter

dewlap – a fold of skin that hangs from the throat of some animals e.g. eland

diurnal – an animal that is active during the day

eco-tourist – someone who travels to wildlife destinations on holiday

endangered – species that are in danger of becoming extinct, and usually protected by law

engravings – art that is cut or carved into a hard surface like stone

excrement – the waste matter discharged from the bowels

exoskeleton – the hard, external covering, especially of insects

extinction – the final loss of an entire species that will never exist in living form again

fault – a break in the earth's layers of rock caused by movement of the earth's crust

forage – to search for food

gabions – rocks that are packed together in wire mesh, in order to prevent soil being washed away

gape – the angle at base of bill where upper and lower parts of the mouth meet

glaciers – a river of ice that moves very slowly

gradient – the steepness of a hill or mountain

grazers – animals that mainly eat grass and roots

gregarious – living in social groups

habitat – the natural environment of an animal or plant

hierarchy – a system that ranks one animal above another

indigenous – plants that are native to an area ie. were not brought in from another area

initiation – a special ceremony that admits a person into the society as an adult

insectivorous/insectivore – an animal that eats insects

invasive – plants that spread easily into an area where they are not wanted

kraal – an enclosure for goats, sheep and cattle

larva – an insect, from time of leaving egg, until changing into pupa

latex – the milky liquid in the stems and leaves of certain plants

linguistic group – a group of people who speak the same language

matriarch – a female that is the leader of her herd, pride or flock

migrant – a bird that moves to warmer areas when it gets cold and food is scarce

millenium – a period of 1000 years

minerals – non-living material which occurs naturally in the earth, often in rocks

molten – rock which has been made liquid by great heat

neurotoxic – poisonous or destructive to the nervous system

nocturnal – an animal that is active during the night

nomadic – people who move from place to place seeking new pasture or hunting grounds

nursery herd – a herd of female antelope with young, living together after breeding season

nutrients – natural elements which create richer soil

nutritious – high quality food

nymph – the immature stage of some insects

ochre – a yellow, red or brownish mineral made of clay and iron oxide, used as a colouring

omnivorous/omnivore – an animal that eats meat and plants

palatable – grass which is nutritious

perennial – water which lasts all year round

pheromone – a chemical substance released by an animal which affects sexual behaviour

pioneer plant – the first plants to grow in disturbed soil with very little nutrients

plumage – a bird's feathers, particularly in breeding season

predator – an animal (carnivore) that hunts and kills other creatures for food

primate – a specific type of mammal e.g. monkey, baboon

proboscis – elongated mouth part of some insects, used for sucking

quarantined – to isolate animals that may be infected with disease

reservoir – a source of water

rhizome – a modified stem that grows horizontally underground, sending out roots and shoots

rift – a deep crack in the earth

ring-bark – to cut the bark right around the tree eventually killing it

riverine – an area beside a river where the trees are usually evergreen and dense thickets grow

rodent – a small mammal that only has cutting teeth and usually lives on plants

roost – a place where birds perch or settle to sleep

sanctuary – an area where wildlife is protected

scent-mark – the way in which animals mark their territories using urine, spray or dung

scrotum – the pouch in a male mammal containing the testes

silting up – when fine particles of solid matter build up in water and block the flow of water

smelted – the heating and melting of rock so as to obtain the metal inside

solitary – an animal that generally chooses to live alone

subcontinent – a large landmass like southern Africa that forms part of the whole continent

succulent – juicy plants that contain a lot of moisture

tandem – a situation where animals arrange themselves, one behind the other

tanning – to treat the hide of an animal and convert it into leather

territorial – an animal that defends a particular area against rivals of its own species (usually the same sex)

toxin – a poisonous substance

trance – a dream-like state

translocation – the moving of animals from one area or park to another

transpiration – the act of giving off watery vapour from the surface of leaves

turbulence – a state of unrest

ultraviolet rays – certain rays of the sun that are harmful to the skin and eyes

veterinary control – the control and treatment of animal diseases by a skilled vet

waterlogged – areas that become soaked with water after good rains

weir – a small dam built across a stream or river, so that water-flow can be controlled

Species Details

Common Names
The Tswana names of the species, where possible, have been written in brackets. Tswana is the language of the majority of the inhabitants of the North West Province in the area of Pilanesberg.

Scientific Names
These Latin names are written in italics below the common names.

Scientific Data

Trees & plants
- Height is measured in metres or centimetres
- National tree numbers are given in brackets

Mammals
- Height or length are measured in centimetres or metres
- Height (H) is ground to shoulder
- Length (L) is tip of nose to tip of tail

Reptiles & insects
- Length is measured in millimetres, centimetres or metres

Birds
- Length is measured in centimetres from beak-tip to tail-tip, or beak-tip to toe-tip (whichever is longer)
- Roberts bird numbers are given in brackets

Lithographic Repro Three White Dogs, Johannesburg
Printing Fishwick Printers, Durban.

Special thanks
Clive Webber (Johannesburg College of Education), Val Purves (Golden Leopard), Gert Brummer (Stocks and Stocks Leisure), Glynis & Alistair Clacherty (Clacherty & Ass), Joe Moser (Friends of Pilanesberg), Chris Lee (Friends of Pilanesberg), Rick Matthews, Satellite Applications Centre, Frieda Kilian and the reviewers

Jacana Team
Maren Bodenstein, Heather Brooksbank, Carol Broomhall, Miranda Cuefer, Amanda de Lilly, John Dobson, Ryan Francois, Liz Godfrey, Zann Hoad, Nafeesa Karim, Mirela Kerns, Wendy Madsen, Malvina Mayaba, Maisie Mbali, Andrea Meeson, Obed Molobe, Remmington Motloung, Debbie Munro, Fortune Ncube, Mpume Ncube, Davidson Ndebele, Dave Ngwenya, Eric Ngwenya, Jenny Prangley, Angela Price, Joan Sibiya, Natasha Stretton, Peter Thomas, Val Thomas, Pam Thompson, Lauren Witten.

Created by Jacana
All rights reserved.
No part of this publication may be reproduced, adapted, stored in a retrieval system, or transmitted in any form or by any means, electronic, mechanical, photocopying, recording, or otherwise, without the written permission of the copyright owner.
The publisher welcomes any comments.
Published by
© Jacana Education Johannesburg 1997
P.O. Box 2004, Houghton 2041, Republic of South Africa
1st Edition 1997
2nd Edition 1998
ISBN 1-874955-54-9

PILANESBERG

A Complete Guide to the Park

This book will give you a broader, and more detailed, insight into the fascinating world of wildlife here.

There is far more to the Pilanesberg than just finding lions!

Pilanesberg is one of the oldest and largest volcanic complexes on earth.

You may find...
the largest, or the fastest, or one of the most endangered land mammals on earth; or the largest flightless bird, just one of over 300 species of birds in the Park; or some of the thousands of plant, insect or reptile species.

Of course, one can never hope to see it all, but Pilanesberg's magic will be found in its unique geology, its ancient and extraordinary history, in the diversity of life and in looking for the big game.

One of the best wildlife experiences that you can hope for is waiting for you, if you know where and how to look.

Use this book to help you.

CONTENTS

VOLCANOES AND ROCKS

Birth of Pilanesberg   Pages 2 - 5

These pages take us back 1300 million years, when the volcano erupted. Travelling inside the ancient volcano, you will discover how and why Pilanesberg's geology is so varied and unusual.
These pages tie in with the Geological Sites in the Park – see pages 50 - 57. Use the Map on pages 48 - 49.

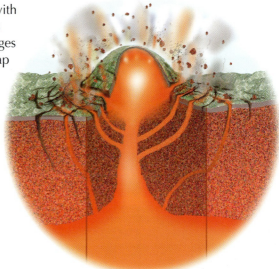

FORMATION OF NATURAL HABITATS   Pages 6 - 11

Once the volcano stopped blasting the area into new shape, time slowly started transforming Pilanesberg, and life settled down in this natural sanctuary. The forces of nature gradually changed the landscape and created the habitats we see today. Man-made areas have also been created – dams are now the lifeblood of the Park, and roads have attracted many specific species. The formation of natural and man-made habitats is a never-ending process.

Hillside and Grassland	*Page 6*
Thickets	*Page 8*
Rocky Areas	*Page 10*
Dams and Roads	*Page 11*

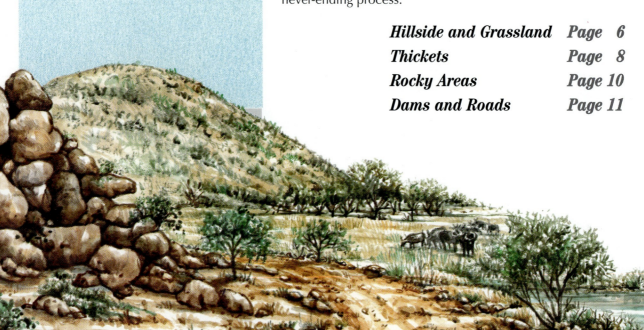

Contents

SPECIES GUIDE Pages 12 - 35

Animal and plant species have been grouped in the habitats where you are *most likely* to find them. But remember that habitats merge into one another and different species also move through different habitats all the time. Use these pages as a broad guide only.

Hillside	*Page 12*
Grassland	*Page 14*
Thickets	*Page 18*
Rocky Areas	*Page 24*
Water Areas	*Page 28*
Sand Roads	*Page 32*
Large Birds	*Page 34*

NIGHT SPECIES

Experience a Different World   *Page 36*

Nocturnal species have adapted to being active at night. You can sometimes see them at dawn or dusk, but the best time to look for these exciting animals is on an official night drive.

HISTORY

Humans and Nature   *Pages 38 - 41*

People, plants and animals lived side by side in the Pilanesberg for millions of years. At first the humans were hunted by predators. Then we invented tools and weapons and we became the hunters.

Over time, we learned to grow crops and keep domestic stock. Very recently, mechanised farming and denser populations drove out most wild creatures.
Then came Operation Genesis...

PILANESBERG PARK

Creation and Conservation
Pages 42 - 43

In 1979 when the Park was started, Operation Genesis was the largest game translocation ever. People began to help wild species to re-establish and Pilanesberg now is a triumph of nature.

However it is visited by thousands of people every year. It therefore has to be managed to ensure that natural balances continue to be restored and maintained.

STORIES TOLD BY THE OLD MAN OF MORULENG
Pages 44 - 47

PILANESBERG MAP   *Pages 48 - 49*

POINTS OF DISCOVERY
Pages 50 - 57

SPECIES TICK LIST   *Pages 58 - 59*

INDEX
Pages 60 - 61

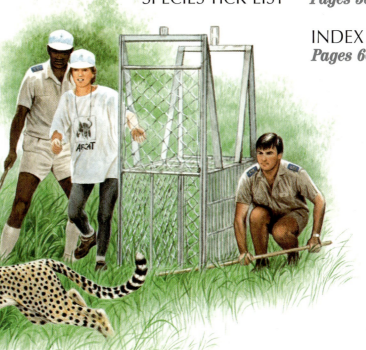

VOLCANOES AND ROCKS

Birth of Pilanesberg

Pilanesberg is one of the largest volcanic complexes of its kind in the world. The rare rock types and structure of the Pilanesberg make it a unique geological feature.

These four pages will take you back into time, to Pilanesberg's violent birth millions of years ago. They explain how it happened and what you can see today, as you drive through the Park.

It is 1300 million years ago. Primitive organisms like algae are the only life-form on earth. It is a hostile place. Strong winds howl, earthquakes and huge volcanic eruptions are common.

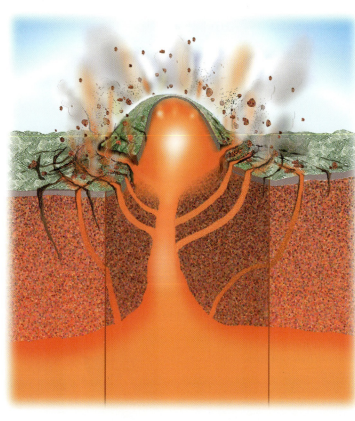

A

Tearing the Earth Apart

The furnace inside the earth is hotter than 1000°C and has caused rocks to melt. This molten rock (magma) floods up the cracks the earthquake has caused. The magma collects in a large pool, called a 'hot spot', just below the crust. It builds up immense pressure against the roof of the magma chamber. (Arrows show direction of flowing magma)

B ### Cracks Release the Fire

This pressure stretches deep circular and radial cracks to split the earth's crust open. When viewed from above, these cracks look like a window that has been hit by a stone (See Satellite photo, page 5). Boiling rock, ash and gas erupt violently into the sky. The rocks at G1 (see Map, Point 5) are from the initial explosions. They are called volcanic rocks.

CUT AND POLISHED ROCK SURFACES FOUND AT GEOLOGICAL SITES IN PILANESBERG TODAY

Birth of Pilanesberg

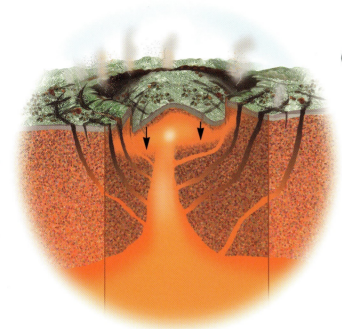

C
The Crust Collapses
When the magma bursts out of its holding chamber, there is no longer any support for the brittle, stretched crust above it. As a result, the crust collapses down into the magma chamber. (Arrows show direction of crust collapsing)

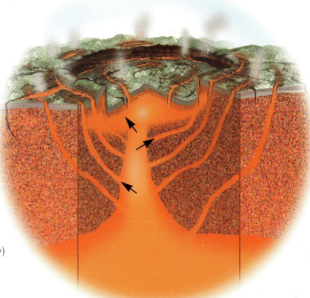

D
Lava Flows Out
When the crust collapses, magma that is still in the chamber is forced upwards. This process is the same as when a cork is pushed into a full bottle of liquid and the liquid and air spurt out. Magma pours out of the cracks and floods the landscape as lava. This lava solidifies into volcanic rocks and remnants of this can be seen at G3 (see Map, Point 12). (Arrows show direction of lava flow)

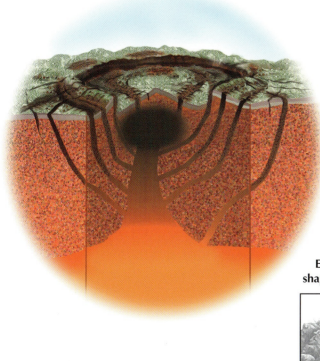

E
Magma Cools and Clogs Up the Cracks
Some magma does not erupt onto the surface as lava. It begins to cool, harden and clog up the cracks inside the earth. It then solidifies into rock formations known as dykes. They consist of rocks called foyaites and syenites. In Pilanesberg, many of these dykes are circular in shape because of the circular cracks and are called ring-dykes. They are especially prominent in the south-west of Pilanesberg. (See Satellite Photo, page 5)

The entire process happened many times during the volcano's active lifespan of about 1 million years. Each time a new set of cracks opens up, different types of magma are released. Different rock types are formed in this way.

Eventually the volcano settles down and time and erosion take over to shape the land into what we see today.

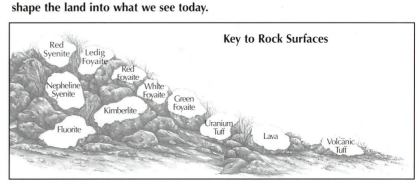

Key to Rock Surfaces

VOLCANOES AND ROCKS
Birth of Pilanesberg
(continued)

How Erosion Reveals the Secrets Inside the Earth
Erosion has exposed the inside of the original volcano and its rocks to us. Today we see what is left after millions of years of weathering.

KEY TO GEOLOGICAL SITES IN THE PARK

Man-made
Old Flourite Mine G8

90 Million Years Old

Kimberlite G4

1300 Million Years Old

Volcanic Rocks

Volcanic Tuff G1
Lava G3
Uranium-bearing Tuff G13

Foyaites

Green Foyaite G6, G10

White Foyaite G5, G14

Red Foyaite G9, G15

Ledig Foyaite G11

Tinguite No G-site

Syenites

Red Syenite G7, G12, G15
Nepheline Syenite G2

2 000 Million Years Old

Pre-volcanic Rocks

Granite and Gabbro - No G-site

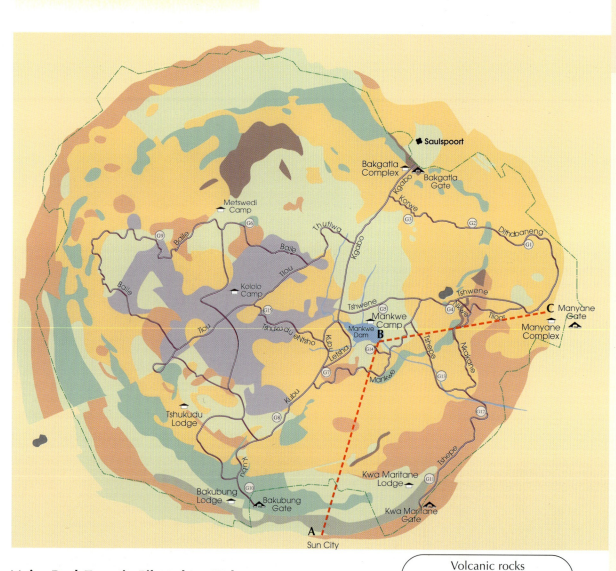

Major Rock Types in Pilanesberg Today
Cross Section (indicated by -----) from Sun City (**A**) through Mankwe Dam (**B**) to Manyane (**C**)

Volcanic rocks (lavas & tuffs) erode much faster than the ring-dykes and outcrops of foyaite and syenite. As a result these erosion-resistant syenites and foyaites stand out prominently.

Birth of Pilanesberg

This satellite photo shows the ring-dyke structure which is more noticeable in the south-west of the complex. It also shows the central rocky outcrops and flatter regions of volcanic rock in the north-east. Millions of years after the volcanic explosions, a crack in the earth's crust cut the Pilanesberg in half, from the south-west to the north-east. Erosion took advantage of this weakness and eventually formed a broad valley across Pilanesberg. Tlou Drive follows some of this eroded fault zone.

KEY	
A	Metswedi Camp
B	Kololo Camp
C	Tshukudu Lodge
D	Bakubung Lodge
E	Bakgatla Complex
F	Mankwe Camp
G	Kwa Maritane Lodge
H	Manyane Complex

Use the Map on pages 48 - 49 to discover more about volcanoes and rocks. These are at marked Geological Sites (G1 – 15) on pages 50 - 57.

Pilanesberg has survived aeons of erosion and stands high above the surrounding bushveld plains. Near the centre stands Thabayadiotso, which is a fitting name, meaning the 'proud mountain'.

The turbulence which formed Pilanesberg has moved away long ago, due to the shifting of the earth's continents. For this reason we can be almost sure, that Pilanesberg will never erupt again.

But the process of erosion continues and so do the cycles of nature in Pilanesberg.

FORMATION OF HABITATS

Hillside and Grassland

Hillside vegetation differs from grassland because the gradient of the slope allows nutrients in the soil to drain to the bottom of the slope. Different soils and the effects of fire also change the vegetation. Grass has relatively little moisture content, and so grassland attracts species which are more dependent on drinking regularly.

Rain
Water from heavy rainstorms washes soil downhill. Natural erosion is caused, especially on the steeper slopes, where faster flowing water carries away large amounts of soil.

South-facing Slopes
Southern slopes are cooler and retain moisture, as they receive less sun. Typical trees found here include the Transvaal beech and the cabbage tree.
(See pages 23 & 24)

Flowing water causes nutrients and soil to drain to the bottom of slopes.

Ouklip
Over decades, as the water from waterlogged areas evaporates, iron-rich minerals are left behind. These bake in the heat of summer. Eventually a hard layer of rock, called ouklip, is formed beneath a layer of top soil. Trees struggle to take root through the hard ouklip layer, but grassland flourishes.

Ouklip

Sweetveld
These lower lying areas become waterlogged in summer. The extra nutrients and water results in the growth of sweetveld. Grazers prefer sweetveld, and it is often over-grazed in summer. As a result, many species move onto hillslopes in winter.

Hillside and Grassland

Sun

Large rocks are broken down by centuries of weathering. Gravity carries them down the slope.

Over thousands of years the rocks are worn down to form soil. These nutrients in the soil feed the plants, which in turn feed the animals.

North-facing Slopes

North-facing slopes receive more sun. They are therefore hotter and drier. As a result they have different vegetation from southern slopes. Some typical trees found here are the red bushwillow and the live-long tree.
(See page 12)

On grassland animals like zebra, wildebeest and tsessebe, evolved in larger herds for two main reasons. Firstly, grassland provides more food per hectare than any other habitat and can sustain large numbers of animals. Secondly, these animals rely on safety in numbers, as it is harder for predators to pick out a single animal from a large herd. These species developed speed and stamina to outrun predators on the open areas.
(See tsessebe page 14)

Two species graze here in smaller groups – the white rhino which lacks speed, but is successful due to its size and strength, and the hippo, which grazes at night.

FORMATION OF HABITATS

Thickets

Thickets provide less food per hectare than grassland. Small groups of browsers that enjoy leaves, thorns, fruit, pods and bark, feed here. Many animals rely on the dense cover of thickets for protection, as well as on camouflage and agility. Small herds can keep together in thickets, even when chased by predators.

Thickets offer safety for mothers and their young. Many species, including the big cats, give birth to young in thickets, keeping them there until they are strong enough to move into more open areas.

Gully Thickets

Erosion wears away gullies and kloofs between hillslopes. These areas are sheltered from the sun and are therefore usually cooler and wetter.

This gives protection against fire and allows dense vegetation to grow.
Gully thickets are remnants of ancient forests which have survived dry periods due to the shade, protection and greater moisture there.

The safety of taller trees, and easy availability of food, attracts a wide variey of birdlife, especially forest birds.

Browsers gain much of their water requirements from fleshy, succulent leaves. These animals have slimy, thick saliva which helps them deal with plant toxins, rough thorns and bark.

Termitaria Thickets

Old termite mounds often have trees growing from them. These are known as termitaria thickets. Termitaria are extremely rich in nutrients from the food and excrement of the termites. The channel-ways inside the mound act as a good reservoir for water. Seeds are carried in by wind or birds. The rich, moist soil enables seeds to take root easily here.

Thickets

Sun

Rain

After thousands of years of weathering and gravity, rocks tumble down slopes and break up to form soil.

Break-of-slope Thickets

Vital minerals, nutrients and water collect at the bottom of a slope. This provides deeper soil and more moisture for 'break-of-slope' thickets to grow.

Due to the density of thickets, plants here are protected from extreme weather conditions, especially frost. For this reason plants in thickets are still quite nutritious in winter, and are preferred by many browsers at that time of year.

Riverine Thickets

Underground and surface streams and waterlines, often result in riverine thickets. In winter, plants keep their nutritional value due to these underground water sources.

FORMATION OF HABITATS

Rocky Areas

Rocky outcrops in the Park consist mainly of foyaites and syenites. These rocks are harder than most, and therefore do not erode as quickly as other rocks. As a result, Pilanesberg's rocky outcrops stand out prominently. Species, like the klipspringer and leopard, have adapted to this specialised habitat.

Wind, rain, sun, fire and chemical action erode rocks over centuries. This weathering, as well as the force of gravity, eventually loosens large boulders. They tumble down, break up and finally become soil.

Soil, water and minerals flow between rocks, and collect in basins and pockets along the way. At first pioneer plants grow, improving soil conditions. Decaying matter from these plants enriches the soil, so that other more permanent species can grow, later on.

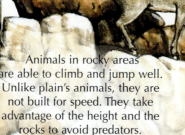

Seeds blown by wind, or carried by birds or animals, come to rest in these fertile, moist pockets of soil. Rocky areas also create favourable conditions for plants to grow by being well sheltered and less susceptable to fire.

Red Balloon Tree seed-pod (see Map; Point 30)

Animals in rocky areas are able to climb and jump well. Unlike plain's animals, they are not built for speed. They take advantage of the height and the rocks to avoid predators.

Rocks absorb heat in the day and give off warmth at night. Reptiles bask on warm rocks to regulate body temperature.

Caves and crevices provide excellent shelter and protection from danger.

Most animals that live in rocky areas do not depend on daily water. Their food provides them with enough moisture.

FORMATION OF HABITATS

Dams and Roads

Man-made habitats have also attracted certain animals and plants.

Dams have given Pilanesberg water all year round and have provided visitors with attractive viewing sites.

Roads are used by many species and they allow visitors to view nature at close range, without damaging or disturbing it.

All streams and rivers in Pilanesberg, arise within the Park itself. They are therefore pollution-free. No rivers here are perennial and they flow only in a wet summer when they refill dams.

Streams from gullies and hillslopes run onto flat areas and natural depressions in the landscape. Some of these natural catchment areas are perfect sites for dams to be built. Dams ensure there is some water during very dry periods.

A smaller dam upstream acts as a filter and prevents the lower dam from silting up. Deposits of silt allow reeds to establish. These also act as a filter and slow down the flow of water helping it to last longer. The result is clearer, cleaner water in the lower dam.

Many animals, especially predators like lions, use man-made roads for easier access. Predators can walk silently here which helps when stalking prey. Roads often stop veld fires from spreading.

Areas with permanent water are well vegetated and therefore attract a diversity of species. Aquatic species, specially adapted to water, live here permanently. These include crabs, fish, aquatic reptiles (like crocodiles and water monitors) and amphibians (like hippos, frogs and terrapins). Dams with islands and dead trees provide safe nesting sites, especially for water-birds.

Water run-off creates dense hedges of vegetation next to the road. However, due to dust thrown up by cars, this is not regularly browsed. These hedges must be controlled by management, to give better visibility to visitors.

Hillside

Red Bushwillow (Mohudiri)
Combretum apiculatum (up to 9 m) (532)
Abundant on rocky, sandy soils; four-winged seeds are slightly toxic and may cause hiccupping, but also used for stomach disorders; wood is very hard; 1 m³ weighs 1300 kg.

Velvet Bushwillow (Mohudiri wa lentsure)
Combretum molle (up to 9 m) (537)
Pale-yellow, sweetly-scented flowers occur on spikes; roots used by local people for snakebite, stomach disorders and fever; red dye is made from leaves.

Large-fruited Bushwillow (Mohudiri)
Combretum zeyheri (up to 12 m) (546)
Leaves and seeds rustle in the winter, hence the common name in Afrikaans – 'raasblaar'; fibrous roots are used for basket weaving; wood is termite and woodborer-proof, so is used for timber.

Live-long (Mmotshwana/Molebatsi)
Lannea discolor (up to 8 m) (362)
Creamy-yellow flowers appear early April; tasty, purple-black fruit; spoons are made from the soft wood.
(See Map, Point 19)

Mountain Reedbuck (Mofele wa thaba/ Mofele o Mohibidu)
Redunca fulvorufula (72 cm H)
Only male has horns; strictly grazers; usually occur in groups of 3 - 6; spend days on rocky slopes, nights on grassy areas near water; lie close together when resting; have shrill alarm whistle.
(See Map, Point 54)

Eland (Phofu)
Taurotragus oryx (170 cm H)
Largest African antelope; distinctive dewlap on the throat and neck hump; primarily browsers, independent of water, getting moisture from roots, tubers and melons; do not sweat thus saving body water; very agile, can clear 2 m fences; females have been known to chase lion away from their young.

Pied Babbler
Turdoides bicolor (26 cm) (563)
Often found in thornveld; moves in noisy groups, calling a high-pitched '*kwee kwee kwee kweer*'; forages on ground for insects.

Crested Barbet (Kokopa)
Trachyphonus vaillantii (23 cm) (473)
Common, colourful bird; perches conspicuously; gives call like an alarm clock lasting about 30 seconds; hops around on the ground with tail and crest erect; bores nesting holes in soft-wood tree trunks, raising up to 4 broods Aug – Feb.

Kudu (Tholo)
Tragelaphus strepsiceros (145 cm H)
Male has long, spiralled horns; almost exclusively browsers with excellent hearing; they are agile and can jump 2 m fences from a standing position; hoarse alarm bark is loudest of the antelope.

Hairy Blue Grass
Andropogon chinensis (1,2 m)

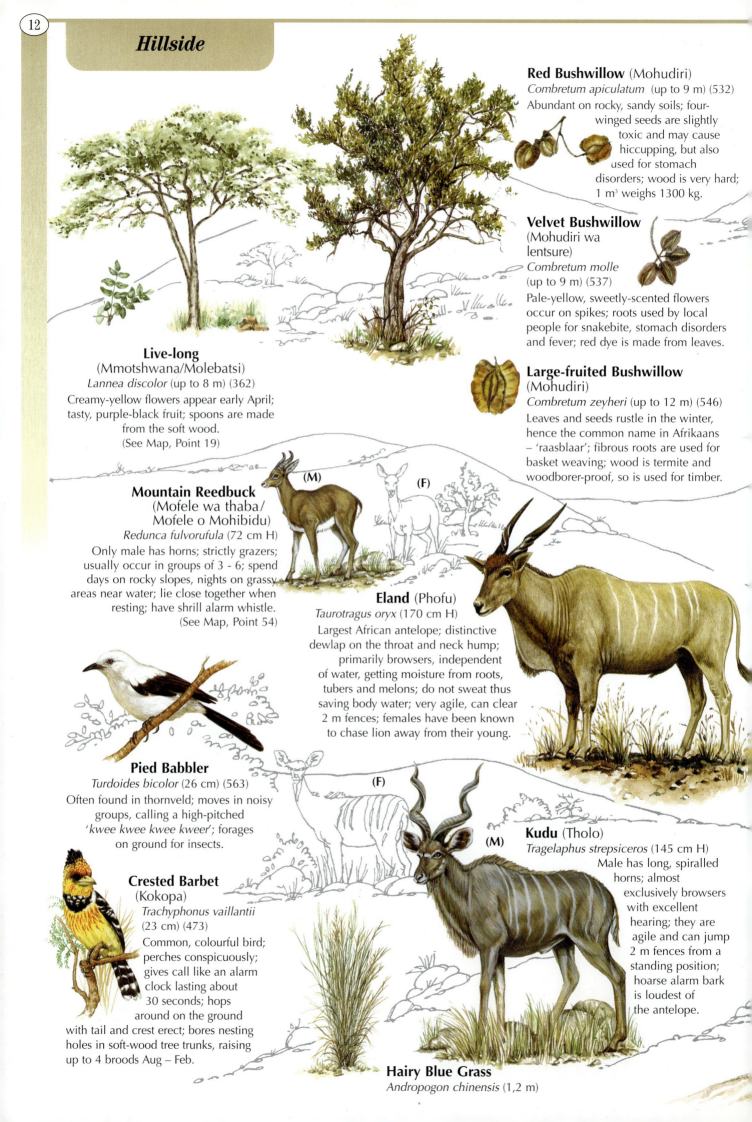

SPECIES GUIDE

Hillside

The process of soil formation starts on hills and mountains. This non-living element is the beginning of all life in the Pilanesberg.

Soil, minerals and nutrients that are washed downhill, feed the plants. This sets thousands of food chains into motion… from herbivores, to great cats, to scavengers, and eventually, back to the soil.

Hillslopes provide food for grazers, browsers and mixed feeders. A wide range of species can be seen here. Some of them may be just passing through to better feeding grounds, or moving to a slope with a more comfortable temperature.

Burchell's Zebra (Pitse e Tilodi)
Equus burchellii (136 cm H)
Most common of the 3 zebra species in Southern Africa; black and white stripes have brown shadow lines; no zebra has same pattern; stripes serve as camouflage, with the herd appearing as one unit, which creates confusion for predators; highly dependent on water; formidable fighters, using teeth and hooves.

Sable Antelope (Kwalata)
Hippotragus niger (135 cm H)
Adult males are darker and have bigger horns; prefer medium-tall grass, drinking water once a day; males are territorial with some in bachelor herds, while dominant cows lead nursery herds; do not usually mix with other animals and most game gives way to them at water.

Rufousnaped Lark
Mirafra africana (18 cm) (494)
Usually seen perched conspicuously, uttering a '*tsee oo*' sound, and rattling wings; dipping flight stops abruptly when it drops into grass and runs in crouched fashion, looking for seeds and insects. Also found in grasslands.

Sabota Lark (Sebota)
Mirafra sabota (15 cm) (498)
Mimics about 60 other species; usually solitary; forages on open ground for insects and seeds; not known to drink water.

Gemsbok (Kukama)
Oryx gazella (120 cm H)
Graze, but also eat roots, bulbs and melons for moisture; will only drink water when available; sometimes eat the soil for minerals; white belly reflects heat from the bare sand which helps regulate body temperature; kidneys concentrate urine so only a few drops are passed.

Golden Beard Grass
Chrysopogon serrulatus (1 m)

Mountain Aloe (Mokgopha)
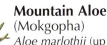
Aloe marlothii (up to 4 m)
Orange flower heads produce nectar popular with sunbirds; leaves used by local people to make snuff and treat roundworm and sunburn.

Grassland

Leadwood (Motswere)
Combretum imberbe (up to 15 m) (539)
Older trees can be recognised by tall trunk, pale-grey, patterned bark and sparse leaves; small four-winged seeds are pale-green; leaves put on a fire to smoke, will relieve coughs & colds; wood is extremely heavy (1 m³ weighs 1 000 kg); prior to metal, indigenous people used the wood for tools and agricultural implements.

Weeping Wattle (Mosetlha)
Peltophorum africanum (up to 10 m) (215)
Could be mistaken for a thorn tree as it has feathery compound leaves, but no thorns; bears large clusters of bright yellow flowers throughout summer; pods are flat and long, hanging in dense clusters; spittle-bug nymph feeding on sap secretes liquid froth, hence the tree appears to be weeping; rarely browsed as leaves cause the stomach contents to froth; great ecological value as bacteria on roots release nitrogen into soil.

Red Hartebeest (Kgama)
Alcelaphus buselaphus (1,2 m H)
Conspicuous white patches on rump; can live without water, grazing almost exclusively; when threatened jump stiff-leggedly with all 4 feet off the ground (pronking); very fast animal, can outrun pursuers; mother conceals newborn calf, returning to feed it and eat its faeces and urine which attract predators.

Tsessebe (Tshesebe)
Damaliscus lunatus (1,3 m H)
White on rump is not as prominent as hartebeest; unlike hartebeest, they drink regularly; grazers, preferring grassy areas surrounded by woodland; regarded as the fastest antelope in southern Africa, reaching speeds of 60 km/h; calves join the herd almost immediately after birth.

Springbok (Tshepe)
Antidorcas marsupialis (75 cm H)
Occur in herds; well adapted to hot arid regions as not dependent on water; browse and graze new grass, flowers and bulbs; adults 'pronk' when danger threatens (bound around on stiff legs, backs arched); young copy adults to give vent to energy.

Black-backed Jackal (Phokojoe)
Canis mesomelas (38 cm H)
Pairs mate for life; males and females defend territory against competitors; efficient hunters, killing young antelope, rodents, hares, birds, reptiles, fish and insects; also eat fruit and berries; follow predators to scavenge.

Cheetah (Lengau)
Acinonyx jubatus (80 cm H)
Prefer open country, have keen eyesight for hunting in daylight; sleek, elongated bodies and semi-retractable claws are adaptations for speed; fastest land-mammal on earth with estimated top speed of about 100 km/h; cubs resemble honey badgers, which possibly deters predators.

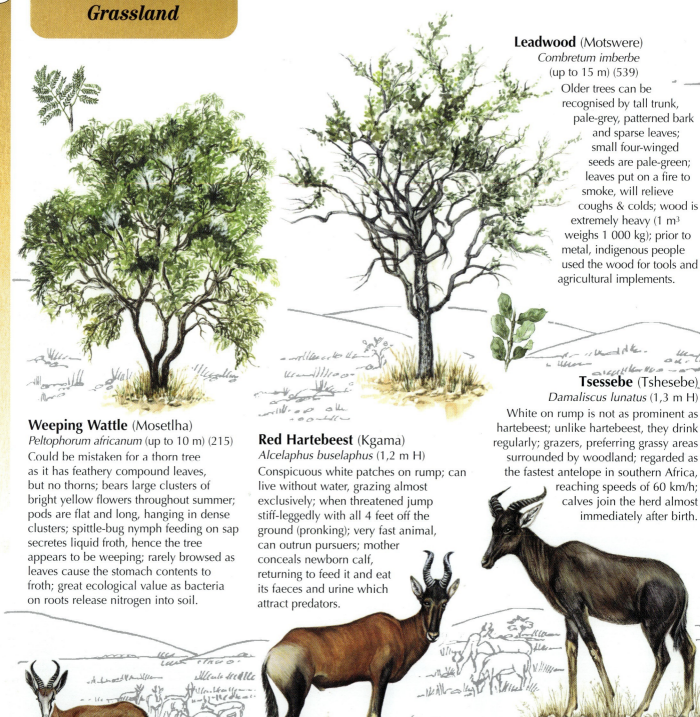

SPECIES GUIDE
Grassland

In the wet summer months, water runs off surrounding hills and the flatter savannah areas become waterlogged. This means there will be enough grazing when the season ends. The wide open grasslands invite larger herds of grazers. They have adapted to their environment and are built for speed and stamina to protect them from powerful predators like cheetah and lion. Longer grass helps the hunters but the good visibility of open plains is an advantage to the hunted. Tactics, stealth and speed decide who wins the day.

Lion (Tau)
Panthera leo (1,2 m H)
Territorial males usually have large manes which develop from 6 months old and serve as protection against bites and blows; lioness does most of the hunting; social animals that observe a strict hierarchy within the pride – adult males often eat first followed by females and cubs; when food is scarce, cubs are unable to compete with adults, often starving to death (up to 80% mortality rate).

Narrow-leaved Turpentine Grass
Cymbopogon plurinodis (30 cm)

White Rhinoceros (Tshukudu e Tshweu)
Ceratotherium simum (1,8 m H)
Heavier than black rhino; mouth wide and square; feeds on short grass in open areas; lives in family groups; poor eyesight but acute hearing and smell; when threatened, put their rumps together facing outwards; newborn calf will follow behind mother, but after a few weeks, it will run ahead.

Blue Wildebeest (Kgokong e pududu)
Connochaetes taurinus (1,5 m H)
Gregarious; territorial males rub facial glands on tree trunks or mark territory on the ground; short-grass grazers, therefore often seen with zebra, impala and giraffe which eat the taller grasses; they also rely on other animals' eye-sight and alertness; pregnant female separates herself from herd to give birth; calves, mobile within minutes of birth, are ready to join the herd within 1 - 2 days.

Wire Grass
Elionurus muticus
(1 m)

Grassland

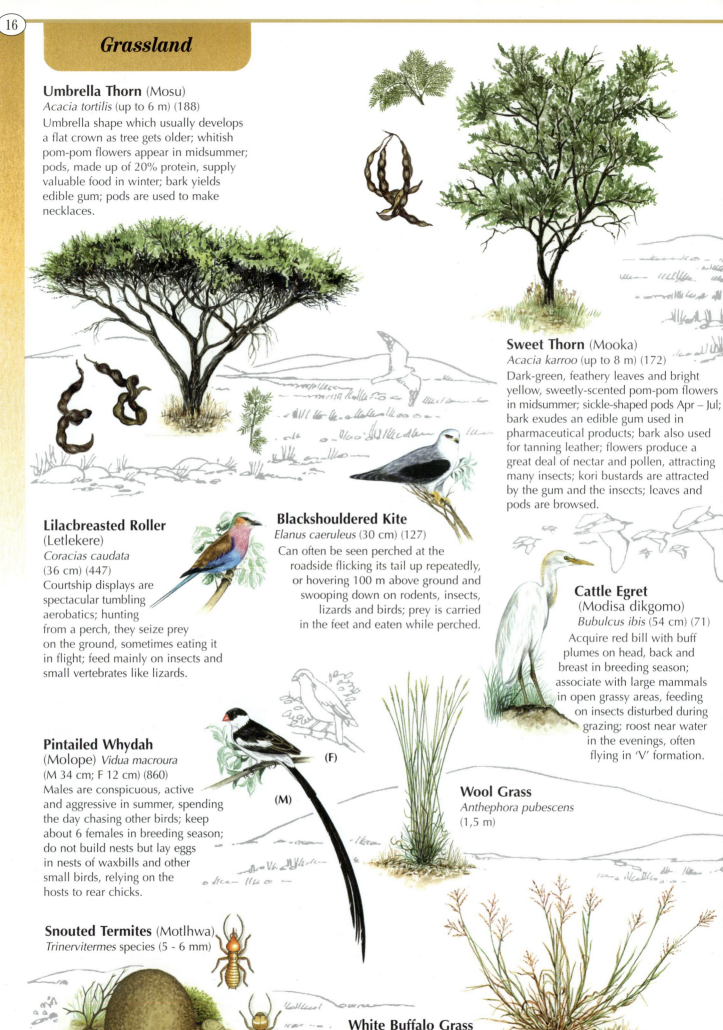

Umbrella Thorn (Mosu)
Acacia tortilis (up to 6 m) (188)
Umbrella shape which usually develops a flat crown as tree gets older; whitish pom-pom flowers appear in midsummer; pods, made up of 20% protein, supply valuable food in winter; bark yields edible gum; pods are used to make necklaces.

Sweet Thorn (Mooka)
Acacia karroo (up to 8 m) (172)
Dark-green, feathery leaves and bright yellow, sweetly-scented pom-pom flowers in midsummer; sickle-shaped pods Apr – Jul; bark exudes an edible gum used in pharmaceutical products; bark also used for tanning leather; flowers produce a great deal of nectar and pollen, attracting many insects; kori bustards are attracted by the gum and the insects; leaves and pods are browsed.

Lilacbreasted Roller (Letlekere)
Coracias caudata (36 cm) (447)
Courtship displays are spectacular tumbling aerobatics; hunting from a perch, they seize prey on the ground, sometimes eating it in flight; feed mainly on insects and small vertebrates like lizards.

Blackshouldered Kite
Elanus caeruleus (30 cm) (127)
Can often be seen perched at the roadside flicking its tail up repeatedly, or hovering 100 m above ground and swooping down on rodents, insects, lizards and birds; prey is carried in the feet and eaten while perched.

Cattle Egret (Modisa dikgomo)
Bubulcus ibis (54 cm) (71)
Acquire red bill with buff plumes on head, back and breast in breeding season; associate with large mammals in open grassy areas, feeding on insects disturbed during grazing; roost near water in the evenings, often flying in 'V' formation.

Pintailed Whydah
(Molope) *Vidua macroura*
(M 34 cm; F 12 cm) (860)
Males are conspicuous, active and aggressive in summer, spending the day chasing other birds; keep about 6 females in breeding season; do not build nests but lay eggs in nests of waxbills and other small birds, relying on the hosts to rear chicks.

Wool Grass
Anthephora pubescens
(1,5 m)

Snouted Termites (Motlhwa)
Trinervitermes species (5 - 6 mm)

White Buffalo Grass
Panicum coloratum
(1,5 m)

SPECIES GUIDE
Grassland (continued)

Marula (Morula)
Sclerocarya birrea (up to 10 m) (360)
Sweet-smelling fruit, occuring in late summer, is rich in Vitamin C making a refreshing drink, an alchoholic brew, a tasty jelly and jam; elephant do not become intoxicated from eating the fermenting fruit, but baboons, with smaller body weight, may be affected; seeds inside taste like walnuts and contain oil used in indigenous cosmetics; bark contains a substance that can treat blisters caused by hairy caterpillars; timber being tough is used for many purposes; roots and leaves are valuable game fodder; Venda people make a bark mixture used to determine the sex of an unborn child. (See Map, Point 17)

Fine Thatching Grass
Hyparrhenia filipendula
(1,5 m)

Buffalo (Nare)
Syncerus caffer (1,5 m H)
Males have large horns with heavier bosses than females; grazers, but browse if grass is scarce; adult bulls often wallow in mud; not territorial, but form large herds with bulls sometimes breaking away into bachelor herds; acute sense of smell; normally docile but old bulls have been known to kill lion; extremely dangerous when wounded.
(See Map, Point 46)

Blackbreasted Snake Eagle (Ntsu)
Circaetus gallicus/pectoralis (68 cm) (143)
Can be confused with the martial eagle, but is smaller and in flight has white undersides with dark stripes on wings and tail; bare black and yellow legs; hovers and swoops down when a snake is sighted, kills it and eats it in flight.

Gum Grass
Eragrostis gummiflua
(90 cm)

Thickets

Wild Olive (Motlhare)
Olea europaea/africana (up to 7 m) (617)
Common, widespread tree; smooth, shiny dark-green leaves; purple-black, bitter fruits are eaten by animals; wood was used for ornaments. (See Map, Point 61)

Jacket-plum/Indaba Tree (Mopepenwe)
Pappea capensis (up to 10 m) (433)
Hardy, evergreen tree with rough, leathery leaves; soft, hairy berries which split like a jacket to reveal a soft red seed capsule; fleshy part is browsed; used to make jelly and alcoholic beverage; Cecil John Rhodes and Matabele chief Lobengula, met under one of these trees, hence 'Indaba tree'.

Common Duiker (Phuti/Photi)
Sylvicapra grimmia (52 cm H)
Solitary browsers showing preference for tips of plants; rarely drink water; most active at night or cooler parts of day; rely on keen senses of smell and vision; freeze in danger, flee in ducking, zig-zag manner.

Tree Squirrel (Setlhora)
Paraxerus cepapi (35 cm L, including tail)
Nest in old barbet or woodpecker nests; feed on ground during the day; female produces 2 young, which remain in tree-hole until able to climb up and down; eat fruit, nuts and sometimes insects; enemies are birds of prey, genets and pythons; when meeting a snake they mob it hysterically.

Vervet Monkey (Kgabo)
Cercopithecus aethiops (114 cm L)
Sociable animals which groom each other to remove pests and strengthen bonds; adult male has blue scrotum; prefer fruit and pods, but also eat insects, eggs and small birds; main enemies are leopards and eagles.

Steenbok (Phudufudu)
Raphicerus campestris (52 cm H)
Solitary or in pairs in established territories; depend on water; when threatened, flee in a zig-zag run, then stop to glance back; young hidden for a few weeks; lie motionless when approached; martial eagles prey on the young.

Tropical Tent Spider (Segokgo)
Cyrtophora species (8 - 20 mm)

Golden Brown Baboon Spider (Tshere)
Pterinochilus species (60 mm)

Guinea Grass
Panicum maximum (2,5 m)

Spotted Bush Snake (Legwere)
Philothamnus semivariegatus (70 - 100 cm; max 126 cm)

SPECIES GUIDE

Thickets

For thousands of years specific animals have adapted perfectly to this habitat. It is suited to browsers, who have learned to use camouflage and secrecy, for protection. Carnivores, like the smaller cats, hunt here. They rely on surprise attacks, rather than the fast chases of the lioness and cheetah.

Taller trees grow in riverine areas, kloofs and gullies, where water and soil collect. This provides perfect nesting sites for birds, and offers the safety and food required for animals in the breeding season… …watch carefully for the black rhino and smaller shy antelope, but especially for the many different birds that inhabit these areas.

Buffalo-thorn (Mokgalo)
Ziziphus mucronata (up to 9 m) (447)

Shrub or tree with shiny, fresh-green leaves; paired thorns, one straight, one strongly curved; deciduous, but a few leaves remain in winter; heavily browsed; monkeys, baboons and eland eat the berry-like fruit; local people believe in the magical ability to deflect lightning, and ward off evil spirits; a sacred tree to the Zulus; has many medicinal uses.

Black Rhinoceros (Tshukudu e Ntsho)
Diceros bicornis (1,6 m H)

Endangered species; smaller than white rhino with hooked, triangular upper lip adapted for browsing; bite off thick, woody sticks; tolerate thorns and natural chemicals of poisonous plants; solitary and unpredictable with nervous energy and curiosity; babies run behind mothers and therefore fall prey to lion; horns consist of compressed hair, sought after in the East as an aphrodisiac and for dagger handles.

Impala (Phala)
Aepyceros melampus (90 cm H)

Dominant males establish territories and spend rutting season chasing females, grunting and snorting; in breeding season one male dominates breeding herd of females, weaker males group as bachelors; out of season females in nursery herds in loose association with bachelor herds; browse and graze on a wide variety of plants; can jump 3 m high and 12 m in length.

(M)

Bushbuck (Serolobotlhoko)
Tragelaphus scriptus (80 cm H)

Found in thickets near water; males are dark brown, females chestnut; shy and mainly nocturnal; solitary animals or in pairs that browse and graze, picking up fruit and flowers dropped by monkeys and other tree-dwellers; strong swimmers; move to shallow water if threatened; main enemy is the leopard.

(M)

Kraal Spike-thorn
Maytenus polycantha (up to 2 m) (401.2)

Shrub-forming impenetrable thickets used to surround kraals; leaves are small, shiny and grow in clusters; reddish fruit capsules contain yellow seeds.

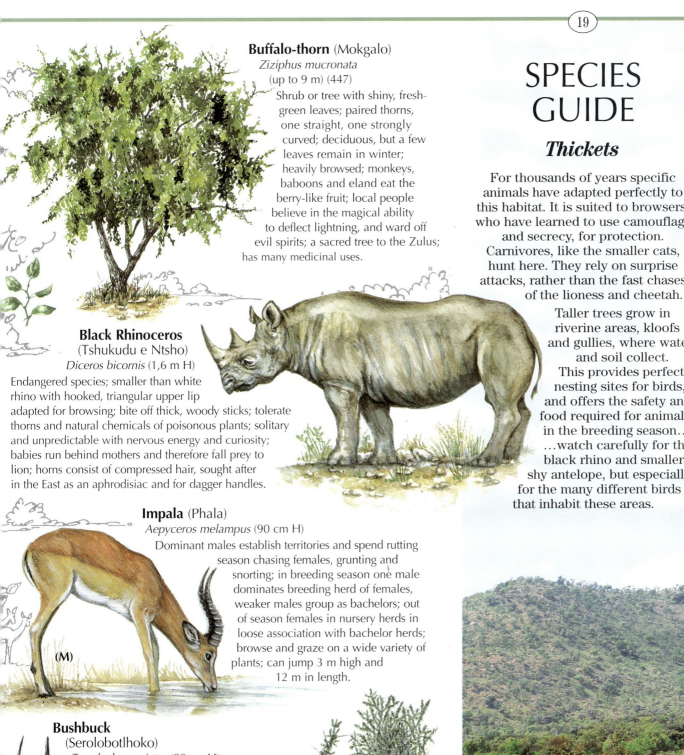

Thickets

Doves (Maeba)
Family Columbidae
Predominantly grey with small heads and stout bodies; fly extremely well but spend much time on the ground picking up seeds which are stored in well developed crops; song is typical coo-ing sound.

Rock Pigeon (Leebarope)
Columba guinea (33 cm) (349)
Nest on cliffs; fly in flocks covering great distances to find food.

Greenspotted Dove (Leeba) *Turtur chalcospilos* (20 cm) (358)

Cape Turtle Dove (Leeba)
Streptopelia capicola (28 cm) (354)

Laughing Dove (Tsokwane)
Streptopelia senegalensis (25 cm) (355)

Hornbills (Dikorwe)
Family Bucerotidae
Nest in holes in tree trunks, with the female sealed inside with only a slit for the male to pass food through; after 20 days, female breaks out, the chicks reseal the nest and are fed by both parents; ungainly looping flight.

Redbilled Hornbill (Korwe)
Tockus erythrorhynchus (46 cm) (458)

Yellowbilled Hornbill (Korwe)
Tockus flavirostris (55 cm) (459)

Blackcollared Barbet (Kokopa)
Lybius torquatus (20 cm) (464)
Sexes alike; usually in pairs but also in larger groups making raucous noise; eat fruit and insects; also found in riverine areas.

Num-num (Morokolo)
Carissa bispinosa (up to 2 m) (640.2)
Small, evergreen shrub with green, new stems and Y-shaped (twice-forked) thorns; leaves are shiny and sharp-tipped; edible, delicious, red berries.

Glossy Starling (Legodi)
Lamprotornis nitens (24 cm) (764)
Small flocks; pair off in breeding season; distinctive 'turr treau' call; feed on insects, fruit and aloe nectar; fond of camp titbits.

Arrowmarked Babbler (Letsheganoga)
Turdoides jardineii (24 cm) (560)
Move around from tree to tree in noisy groups of about 10; feed mainly on insects, also spiders, small reptiles and fruit; about 7 birds help to build nest.

Whitebrowed Robin
Erythropygia leucophrys (15 cm) (613)
Usually seen singly or in pairs on ground or in scattered scrub; make varied, clear calls from tree-tops; 2 - 3 eggs laid on ground Oct – Dec.

Helmeted Guineafowl
(Kgaka) *Numida meleagris* (58 cm) (203)
Roost in trees at night; congregate in large flocks on the ground where they forage for seeds, bulbs and insects; have been seen removing ticks from warthogs.

Red Toad
(Segwagwa) *Bufo carens* (7 cm L)
Abundant towards end of summer; travel far in search of a dark, quiet place to spend the winter – shoes left in cupboards often serve this purpose well!

SPECIES GUIDE
Thickets (continued)

Giraffe (Thutlwa)
Giraffa camelopardalis (3,3m)
Tallest mammal; weighs up to 2 000 kg; browse over 100 tree species, especially thorn-trees; not dependant on daily water; non-territorial, living in loose social system; known to eat bones for extra calcium.

Stink Shepherd's Tree (Motlopi)
Boscia foetida (up to 5m) (124,127)
Inner wood and flowers (Aug – Sept) have rancid smell, hence common name; edible fruit. (See Map, Point 4)

Garbage Line Spider (Segokgo)
Cyclosa species (50 - 150 mm)

Golden Orb Web Spider (Segokgo)
Nephila senegalensis (25 - 30 mm)

Tropical House Gecko (Separela-Nkong)
Hemidactylus mabouia mabouia (12 - 15 cm)

Elephant (Tlou)
Loxodonta africana (3,2 - 4m H)
Bulls have rounded foreheads whereas cows' are angular; have an acute sense of smell and hearing but limited sight; often a preference for left or right, shown by one tusk being more worn than the other; herds are lead by matriarchs; bulls are solitarily or in bachelor herds; eat about 300 kg of food, and drink about 160 litres of water a day; although they damage trees, this helps create low growth for smaller browsers; visitors must approach with caution, especially breeding herds.

Thickets

Black Thorn (Mongana)
Acacia mellifera (up to 8 m) (176)
Tree or shrub forming impenetrable thickets; creamy-white pom-pom flowers in spring; good firewood. (See Map, Point 26)

Puzzle Bush (Morobe)
Ehretia rigida (up to 4 m) (657)
Common shrub with tangled appearance; clusters of sweetly-scented, lilac flowers Aug – Feb; branches are used in cattle kraals, as they are believed to subdue bad-tempered oxen; hunters used to believe that pointing these branches at animals will render them weak.

Cardinal Woodpecker (Kokopa)
Dendropicos fuscescens (15 cm) (486)
Often heard making rapid tapping noises on branches; usually work a tree from bottom up to the top, looking for grubs and insects; excavate holes in dead trees for nesting.

Redbilled Woodhoopoe
Phoeniculus purpureus (36 cm) (452)
Occur in noisy, restless groups which move from tree to tree, clambering around branches looking for insects, millipedes and small reptiles; they nest in holes made by woodpeckers and barbets.

Crimsonbreasted Shrike
(Mampa tshibidu)
Laniarius atrococcineus (25 cm) (739)
Associated with dry, semi-arid thornveld; vocal birds, seen alone or in pairs, foraging on ground for insects; called 'Reichsvogel' in Namibia as colours are same as the old German flag.

Hoopoe (Pupupu)
Upupa epops (26 cm) (451)
Walks about probing the ground for insects; will sometimes extract insects from the bark of trees; flies in a butterfly fashion; its call is a monotonous 'hoo poop poop'; smelly nest as they do not remove faeces.

Fiscal Shrike (Tlhomedi)
Lanius collaris (23 cm) (732)
Hunt from perches carrying prey in beaks or feet; sometimes hang prey on thornbushes or fences, returning later to feed, hence the name 'butcher bird'.

Firefinches
Family Estrildidae
Gregarious; feed on ground for seed, often at water; host to widow finches, incubating and rearing their young.

Redbilled Firefinch
Lagonosticta senegala (10 cm) (842)

Jameson's Firefinch
Lagonosticta rhodopareia (11 cm) (841)

Blackheaded Oriole
Oriolus larvatus (25 cm) (545)
Utters beautiful, liquid call from tops of tall trees; mainly insectivorous, but will feed on fruit and nectar; it makes a deep well-concealed, moss nest, lined with spider webs and plant material.

Blackeyed Bulbul
(Rankolokota)
Pycnonotus barbatus (22 cm) (568)
Abundant and common in variety of habitats; gregarious, cheerful, vocal and active; eat insects, fruit and nectar; call sounds like, 'Wake up Gregory'.

Forktailed Drongo
(Kuamesi)
Dicrurus adsimilis (25 cm) (541)
Immature birds have white wingpatches, flashed in flight, but adults are totally black; perch at tops of trees; are aggressive, often harassing birds of prey; mimic other birds but main call is a rasping squeak; catch insects in the air, mob other birds, and also eat small birds and sometimes fish.

SPECIES GUIDE
Thickets
(continued)

Transvaal Beech (Mofufu/Monyena)
Faurea saligna (up to 8 m) (75)
Also commonly found on hillsides; long, slender leaves on droopy branches, turning red in autumn; white-mauve flowers hang in spikes from Aug – Jan;. (See Map, Point 28)

Grey Lourie (Mokoe)
Corythaixoides concolor (48 cm) (373)
The 'go away' call alerts game when predators approach; perch at tops of trees and fly in laboured fashion; roost in groups at night; usually nest in thorn trees; eat fruit, flowers, buds, leaves, insects and sometimes small birds.

Brownhooded Kingfisher
Halcyon albiventris (24 cm) (435)

Kingfishers
All nest in holes; species vary greatly in size; both these species eat insects.

Striped Kingfisher
Halcyon chelicuti (18 cm) (437)

Marico Flycatcher
Melaenornis mariquensis (18 cm) (695)
Perches conspicuously on leafless outer branches of thorn trees, uttering harsh unmusical sound; catches insects on the ground; nest is a shallow bowl of roots and coarse twigs made on a horizontal branch.

Chinspot Batis
Batis molitor (13 cm) (701)
Often hang upside down to remove insects and spiders from leaves; call consists of 3 descending syllables, sounding like 'three blind mice'.

Speckled Mousebird (Letsiababa)
Colius striatus (32 cm) (424)
Fruit-eating birds; hang in a vertical position in trees or scramble about in mouse-like fashion; occur in small flocks in dense, moist areas.

Blue Waxbill (Lebibi)
Uraeginthus angolensis (13 cm) (844)
Forage for seed on the ground; drink water regularly; nests sometimes built near wasps for protection; pintailed whydahs lay their eggs in these nests.

Whitebacked Mousebird (Letsiababa)
Colius colius (33 cm) (425)
Occur in drier areas; sometimes forage on ground.

Rocky Areas

Common Tree Euphorbia (Ngoge)
Euphorbia ingens (up to 15 m) (351)
Angular, segmented fleshy branches produce a milky latex causing skin irritation and blindness; poison was used by local people to catch fish. (See Map, Point 34)

Large-leaved Rock Fig (Moumo)
Ficus soldanella (up to 7 m) (63)
The white roots split the rocks open; baboons feed on the fallen figs. (See Map, Point 18)

Klipspringer (Kololo)
Oreotragus oreotragus (60 cm H)
Live in small family groups; mark territory by dung-piles and pheromone secretion from eye-gland; hooves are blunt with long narrow pads to prevent slipping on rocks; coat has course, hollow, flattened hairs which insulate and help to conserve water; rarely drink water; browse on shrubs, fallen leaves, fruit, flowers and pods. (See Map, Point 66)

Klipspringers & Ticks
Certain species of ticks locate scent-marking from eye-gland of klipspringers; wait on twigs for the animal to return to re-scent, then hop on for a bloodmeal!

Cabbage Tree
Cussonia species (up to 10 m) (563, 564)
Also found on hillslopes; large leaves are dark bluish-green and digitate (hand-like) with deep fissures; bark is cork-like; wood used by Zulu people in treatment of malaria; leaves provide valuable source of fodder.

Hard Tick (Dikgofa)
Rhipicephalus species (3 - 6 mm)

Wall Crab Spider (Flattie) (Segokgo)
Selenops species (15 - 30 mm)
Use lightning speed and camouflage to catch food; keep eggs in white disc-shaped web, woven over small depressions in rock face.

Bristle-leaved Red Top
Melinis nerviglumis (1,2 m)
Leaf sheaths are densely overlapped and hairy with silky pink or white flowering heads; has rolled leaves which help reduce transpiration and conserve water.

SPECIES GUIDE
Rocky Areas

This is the ideal habitat for many different species that have adapted here, because of the safety, food and shelter provided. It is suited to climbing and jumping animals that could not survive in open areas, where speed is needed. Even man was once drawn by these vantage points, from where enemies could be seen, and food easily hunted and gathered.

Rich soil and water collects in crevices and lush vegetation grows. This sets in motion many food chains. Reptiles and dassies bask on rocks, and birds of prey search for them from high above. Baboons come to eat fruit or scorpions, while watching for the leopard. She is lured to caves and secret places to raise her cubs in safety. Perhaps, centuries from now she will still stare across the far valley and in the dead of night, will silently stalk her prey.

Chacma Baboon (Tshwene)
Papio ursinus (1,5 m L)
Largest primate in southern Africa; biggest enemy is the leopard; eats plants, insects, scorpions, fruit, rodents, eggs and even small mammals; highly gregarious, occurring in troops of up to 100 with strict order of dominance; females in season have large crimson backsides and only mate with dominant males; senior males act as sentries and warn other animals of predators.

Common Russet Grass
Loudetia simplex (1,2 m)
Grows in poor, shallow soils in exposed, stony areas and is rarely eaten by animals; flowering heads form attractive golden sprays; often used in thatching and brooms.

Leopard (Nkwe)
Panthera pardus (60 cm H)
Solitary, secretive, nocturnal animals; spend most of the day in hiding; territory is scent-marked with urine; possibly the most dangerous predator when wounded or trapped, using strength, teeth and claws.

Resurrection Plant (Moswiarula)
Myrothamnus flabellifolius (20 - 40 cm)
During winter, this green bush seemingly dies, but miraculously springs to life when given water; has many medicinal uses associated with revitalising the body and treating breast diseases; look out for it on the Nkakane Link. (See Map, Point 22)

Rock Dassie (Pela)
Procavia capensis (54 cm L)
Herbivorous, spending early morning or late afternoon feeding at a furious rate; regularly bask in the sun to increase body temperature; eyesight and hearing acute; very agile with glandular secretions on soles of feet to prevent slipping; it is claimed that they have different alarm calls for eagles, leopards and pythons.

Rocky Areas

Lavender Fever-berry
(Moologa)
Croton gratissimus (up to 2 m) (328)
Common tree with elongated leaves, dark-green on top, silver-white dotted with brown underneath; leaves have a lavender fragrance which San women used for perfume.

Raisin Bush
Grewia species
(up to 4 m) (458, 459, 462, 463)
Rounded stems; yellow flowers produce edible, lobed fruits, reddish when ripe; wood is used for making walking sticks and assegai handles.

Common Wild Pear
(Mokgofa)
Dombeya rotundifolia (up to 7 m) (471)
Common tree; rough sand-papery leaves; clusters of white or pink flowers appear Jul – Sep; extracts of bark, roots and leaves used for stomach ailments and headaches.

Hard Fern
Pellaea calomelanos
Can survive in exposed, hot, dry places among rocks, by shrivelling up in dry times and rehydrating when it rains; leaves used by local people to soothe nerves and treat colds.

Mother-in-law's Tongue
Sansevieria species
Despite its name, is highly prized by man and animal; used in weaving and as a painkiller, worm remedy and treatment for piles and varicose veins; black rhino browse in winter; showy column of flowers; fruits Nov – Feb.

African Rock Python
(Tlhware)
Python sebae natalensis (3 - 5 m L)
Usually hunts at night, detecting warm-blooded prey with heat sensors on its lips; bite is non-venomous, with prey killed by suffocation e.g. birds, reptiles, small mammals, including antelope and monkeys; protected species but vulnerable as skins used in the fashion industry.

Southern Rock Agama
(Rankgatakwane)
Agama atra
(20 - 25 cm L; max 32 cm)

Black Mamba
(Mokwepa)
Dendroaspis polylepis (2,5 - 4,2 m L)
Common snake; can be found sun-bathing on rocks, or travelling swiftly through the grass with coffin-shaped head held high; will readily attack if threatened; neurotoxic venom causes paralysis of victim's lungs with death in hours if not treated with anti-venom; preys on dassies, game-birds, rodents and lizards.

Rock Monitor (Gopane)
Varanus exanthematicus albigularis
(0,7 - 1,3 m L)
Huge lizard, related to the Komodo dragon; feeds on tortoises, eggs, insects, small birds, rodents and carrion; lives in tunnels under rock overhangs or disused animal burrows or termite mounds; it is a protected animal.

SPECIES GUIDE
Rocky Areas (continued)

Rock Martin (Peolwane)
Hirundo fuligula (15 cm) (529)
Small brown swallow with square white spotted tail; often flies around with other swallows feeding on insects; perches on rocks; builds neat cup-like nest of mud against vertical cliffs.

Black Eagle (Ntsu)
Aquila verreauxii (84 cm) (131)
Uncommon, large eagle, totally black, with a white 'V' on the back and rump; yellow feet and cere; live in pairs, forming permanent bonds; nest in winter against sheer cliff faces, utilising the same nest for generations; female lays 2 eggs a few days apart; the older chick kills the younger one; feed mainly on dassies, but also other mammals, terrestrial birds, carrion and rarely reptiles. (See Map, Point 24)

Mocking Chat
Thamnolaea cinnamomeiventris (22 cm) (593)
Vocal birds with a loud melodious song which mimics about 30 other bird calls; occur in small groups; can be seen running around, sometimes raising tails; drop onto insects on the ground from perch, or jump around in trees in search of fruit.

Redwinged Starling (Legodi)
Onychognathus morio (28 cm) (769)
Slender, elegant, glossy black with chestnut coloured wingtips; often found in large flocks of 100 or more; has a varied diet of fruit, insects, reptiles, ticks and aloe nectar.

Silky Bushman Grass
Stipagrostis uniplumis (75 cm)
Erect, tufted grass with attractive, feathery 3-awned flowers; grows on sandy soils and in disturbed areas.

Rock Kestrel
Falco tinnunculus (32 cm) (181)
Can often be seen hovering, then taking prey from the ground; do not build nests, but lay their eggs on ledges, in holes, trees or old nests of other birds; feed on small mammals, lizards, snakes, insects and other birds.

Robber Fly (Seboba)
Family Asilidae (24 mm)
Long hairy flies that patrol the rocks actively; large mobile heads with bulging eyes; they grab victims, stab them with the proboscis and suck them dry.

Lichens
Can survive extreme conditions very well as are superbly adapted to living on rocks; vulnerable to poisoning by accumulated air pollution; one of oldest plant forms on earth.

Water Areas

Karree (Moshabele)
Rhus lancea (up to 7 m) (386)
Spreading, evergreen, frost resistant tree with willow-like appearance; flowers (winter) are yellow-green, in clusters; fruit hangs in tiny grape-like bunches; beer brewed from fermented fruit; tough and durable wood used for fence posts and implement handles.

River Bushwillow (Modubanoka)
Combretum erythrophyllum (up to 10 m) (536)
Tall, spreading tree, usually found along riverbanks; fast growing and drought resistant; four-winged papery seeds remain on tree all year in clusters at tips of branches – they are poisonous and if eaten cause hiccupping; browsed by elephant and giraffe.

Common Reedbuck (Mofele o mohibidu/Motlobo)
Redunca arundinum (90 cm H)
Mothers only suckle babies once a day; baby moves around frequently to avoid predation; prefer tall grass near water and will swim in extreme danger; have sharp alarm whistle, fleeing in rocking-horse motion with tails fanned over backs.

Sumach Bean (Mosidi/Mositsane)
Elephantorrhiza burkei (up to 3 m) (193)
Small deciduous tree or shrub with feathery blue-green *Acacia*-like leaves; large pods can reach 30 cm in length, often splitting and curling in a tight roll; used in the tanning of leather.

Cape Terrapin (Rantlapere)
Pelomedusa subrufa (28 cm L)

Foam Nest Frog (Mololope)
Chiromantis xerampelina (7 - 8 cm L)
The female produces foam into which she lays eggs. Several males may jostle to release sperm over her eggs.

Common Wild Sorghum
Sorghum bicolor (2,5 m)

Emperor Dragonfly (Seboba)
Anax imperator (7 cm)
Fastest insects in the world; often brightly coloured, especially adult males; territorial predators; they fly over water, scooping up insects in specially adapted legs which form a 'basket'; mating pairs fly in tandem; females dip over water, touching the surface and depositing eggs.

Striped Stream Frog (Segwagwa)
Rana fasciata (3,5 cm L)

Water Monitor (Gopane)
Varanus niloticus (1 - 1,4 m L; max 2 m)

SPECIES GUIDE
Water Areas

Where there is temporary or permanent water, species totally dependent on it, will always be close by. Animals like hippo, waterbuck and the water-birds need water daily. They live here relying on the safety, food and drink provided all year round. Many birds breed near permanent water.

Tiny water organisms play a vital role in a food chain that includes insects, frogs, waders and even crocodiles.

Animals that get enough moisture in the summer from pools, puddles, or plants, come down to dams in the dry winter months. Predators wait… and the peaceful scene is sometimes shattered by the thrill of a kill, or the relief of escape.

Hippopotamus (Kubu)
Hippopotamus amphibius (1,5 m H)
Hippos spend most of the day in water; mate, suckle young and walk underwater creating paths that keep waterways open; sensitive skins protected from ultraviolet rays by a reddish oil secretion; highly territorial, they defend pear-shaped home-ranges; graze at night, often covering up to 10 km while eating up to 130 kg of food; responsible for more human fatalities than any other animal in Africa, moving at speeds of 30 km/h.

Finger Grass
Digitaria eriantha (1 m)

Nile Crocodile
(Kwena) *Crocodylus niloticus* (2,5 - 3,5 m L; max 5,9 m)
Oldest surviving animal on earth; inbuilt barometer detects changes in atmospheric pressure; 50 - 70 eggs laid in hole in sand; eggs on top become males due to greater heat; mother carries young in mouth to water, after which they are independent; prey on antelope, fish and any unsuspecting animal at water's edge; they cannot chew.

Common Waterbuck (Pitlhwa)
Kobus ellipsiprymnus (1,3 m H)
Characteristic white ring on rumps; gregarious grazers, browsing occasionally; use water as refuge, sometimes submerging with only nostrils protruding; oily hair aids waterproofing and has a strong turpentine smell.

Water Areas

Tamboti (Morukuru)
Spirostachys africana
(up to 10 m) (341)
Deciduous tree and leaves turn bright red in autumn; dark, straight trunk; finely patterned rough bark; milky sap could cause blindness; inhalation of wood-smoke causes headache, nausea and diarrhoea; moth larvae live in the seeds making them jump; black rhino eat the leaves.
(See Map, Point 15)

Darter
Anhinga melanogaster (79 cm) (60)
Swim submerged with only snake-like necks sticking out; pierce prey underwater with sharp bills, then swallow whole; lack oil glands and often seen drying wings in the sun.

Whitethroated Swallow (Peolwane)
Hirundo albigularis
(17 cm) (520)
Inter-African migrant; seen alone or in pairs, near water, catching insects in air; will often perch on stumps and posts in water.

Hamerkop (Mamasiloanoka)
Scopus umbretta (56 cm) (81)
Stand in shallow water; stir mud with feet, looking for frogs and fish; build huge dome-like nest of reeds, twigs and grass (up to 50 kg); entrance made of weak material giving way under weight of intruding predators.

Spurwinged Goose (Legou)
Plectropterus gambensis (100 cm) (116)
Largest waterfowl in South Africa, up to 10 kg; large flocks in non-breeding season; male has long spurs on wings for fighting; eats grass shoots, tubers, seeds and aquatic plants.

Whitebreasted Cormorant
Phalacrocorax carbo (90 cm) (55)
Largest cormorant in South Africa; flies fast, low over water; swims partly submerged when alarmed; catches frogs, fish and other aquatic animals.

Dabchick (Sefodi)
Tachybaptus ruficollis (20 cm) (8)
Sometimes rears up out of the water, flapping wings in display; will often follow hippo, picking up disturbed insects and tadpoles; absorbs heat in winter by pointing tail to the sun, exposing the black skin.

Egyptian Goose (Legou)
Alopochen aegyptiacus
(70 cm) (102)
Grazes on short, cropped grass and eats insects during the breeding season to boost protein intake; nests in trees or on buildings; chicks plunge from dizzy heights and head straight for water; females utter a honking sound, males wheeze; mate for life.

Whitefaced Duck (Sefodi)
Dendrocygna viduata
(48 cm) (99)
Has a musical 3-note whistle; dives and forages under-water for aquatic plants and insects.

SPECIES GUIDE
Water Areas *(continued)*

African Fish Eagle (Kgoadira)
Haliaeetus vocifer (73 cm) (148)
Spend most of the day perched in trees watching for fish which they scoop out with their feet, in full flight; loud distinctive call made with head thrown back, even in flight; mate for life. (See Map, Point 27)

Pied Kingfisher
Ceryle rudis (28 cm) (428)
The only black and white kingfisher; hover frequently, with long, straight bills pointing downwards, before splashing into water to catch small fish or insects; nest in holes in sandbanks.

Hadeda Ibis
Bostrychia hagedash (76 cm) (94)
Noisy bird uttering a loud *'haaa'* on take-off and characteristic *'ha ha ha di da'* in flight; small flocks roost in trees and forage on ground, probing their bills deep into the soil for insects; also eat spiders, reptiles, crustaceans, earthworms.

Threebanded Plover
Charadrius tricollaris (18 cm) (249)
Fearless bird, venturing among the feet of elephants and buffalo at water's edge; utters a high-pitched *'wheet'* while running around, suddenly stopping to prod the mud for insects and worms; nest is a mere scraping near the waterline with a few stones added; 1 - 3 well-camouflaged eggs laid.

Grey Heron
Ardea cinerea (1 m) (62)
Plain grey underwing in flight; legs and feet turn reddish in breeding season; usually solitary, stabbing at insects, fish, frogs and crabs; will sometimes feed at night; roost communally.

Reeds (Motlhaka)
Phragmites australis (Up to 3 m)

Lesser Masked Weaver (Thaga)
Ploceus intermedius (15 cm) (815)
Males have black masks in breeding season; weave rounded nests with grass ends sticking out and vertical tunnel-entrance; nests often hang over water; will breed in colonies of not more than 10 birds. (See Map, Point 16)

Yellowbilled Duck (Sefodi)
Anas undulata (60 cm) (104)
Dabbles on water, upending itself to find insects and larvae.

Sand Roads

Khaki Weed
Tagetes minuta (up to 2 m)
Exotic pioneer plant from South America often found in disturbed areas; strong-smelling, black, rice-like seeds used to make tea; if rubbed on the skin, the oils are believed to keep ticks away.

Black-jack
Bidens pilosa

Feathered Chloris
Chloris virgata (80 cm)

Buntings
Family Fringillidae
Small, sparrow-like seed-eaters; forage on the ground.

Goldenbreasted Bunting
Emberiza flaviventris (16 cm) (884)
Sings frequently from a perch, call sounding like 'pretty boy'.

Rock Bunting
Emberiza tahapisi (14 cm) (886)
Not as vocal as other buntings, producing a soft 'pee-wee' call.

Francolins (Masogo) Family Phasianidae
Chicken-like birds with short tails; different species can be identified by patterns on undersides and by distinctive calls; males have spurs on back of legs; fly fast over short distances with whirring wings.

Coqui Francolin (Lesogo)
Francolinus coqui (28 cm) (188)

Crested Francolin (Lesogo)
Francolinus sephaena (33 cm) (189)

Swainson's Francolin (Lesogo)
Francolinus swainsonii (38 cm) (199)

Natal Francolin (Lesogo)
Francolinus natalensis (38 cm) (196)

Leopard Tortoise (Khudu)
Geochelone pardalis babcocki (30 - 40 cm L; max 72 cm)

Ants (Ditshoswane)
Family Formicidae
Highly advanced insects; winged male ants die after mating with queen; workers and soldiers are sterile, wingless females; often suck aphids for the sugary sap they secrete, and protect them from other insects in return; Matabele ants can inflict a painful sting; often seen crossing the road in columns, returning home after raiding a termite mound; each ant will carry up to 5 termites; if the column is disturbed, it emits a high-pitched buzzing noise.

Puff Adder (Lebolobolo)
Bitis arietans arietans (60 - 100 cm L)
Exceptionally well camouflaged; slow to move away when threatened, striking with lightning speed when startled or stepped on; potent cytotoxin causes extensive swelling and tissue death – if untreated the victim could lose a limb or die; prey mainly on rodents.

Dung Beetle (Khukhwane ya boloko)
Family Scarabaeidae (5 - 50 mm)
Adults and larvae eat dung balls; larvae eaten by genets, civets and baboons.

Millipede / Songololo (Sebokolodi)
Doratogonus annulipes (20 mm)

Natal Red Top
Melinis repens
(1 m)

Nightshade
Solanum species (up to 50 cm)
Belong to the potato family; flowers may be mauve, yellow or white, usually small, star-shaped or circular; common species include bitter apple, poison apple and wild tomato; spherical yellow-red fruits should all be regarded as poisonous.

Bee-eaters (Merokapula)
Family Meropidae
Feed on insects, especially butterflies, in the air, or they hawk from a perch, usually returning to same perch to eat prey.

Whitefronted Bee-eater (Morokapula)
Merops bullockoides
(23 cm) (443)
Nest colonially in holes along riverbanks.

Little Bee-eater (Morokapula)
Merops pusillus (17 cm) (444)
Solitary nests in a termite mound or sandbank.

Warthog (Kolobe ya Naga)
Phacochoerus aethiopicus (70 cm H)
Males have prominent tusks and 2 pairs of facial warts to protect eyes during fights; tusks used for digging, defence and fighting; often seen running with tails held stiffly upright; not territorial; feed by kneeling on front legs and dig out roots and rhizomes; sensitive to heat, cold and drought – mud wallowing protects against ultraviolet rays and parasites; use old antbear holes for shelter and breeding.

Slender Mongoose (Tshagane)
Galerella sanguinea
(60 cm L, including tail)
Solitary, diurnal; will take to trees when threatened; inquisitive, sometimes standing upright before disappearing with flick of tail; omnivorous; young will often follow their mother in procession; main enemy are large birds of prey.

SPECIES GUIDE
Sand Roads

Though not a natural habitat, roads attract certain animals, for specific reasons. Some, like reptiles and nightjars, enjoy soaking up the heat that roads give off. The ease of walking with fewer obstacles brings out animals, like tortoises and chameleons, that also enjoy the heat.

Seed-eating birds, like francolins and doves, find food easily in the grasses and in the hedges of bush that grow on the sides of roads. In turn, birds of prey watch eagerly for easy pickings on the open area. Scavengers, owls and many other animals come to eat victims of speeding motorists, especially on main roads. Slow driving will give the visitor rewards. In the open space created by the road, you have the opportunity of seeing many smaller animals normally unseen in the dense bush.

Large Birds

Tawny Eagle (Ntsu)
Aquila rapax (70 cm) (132)
Not common in this area but present all year round; make large nests at top of trees in winter; seen in pairs or singly; varied, scruffy plumage; recognised by pale-yellow cere and gape ending just below eye.

Wahlberg's Eagle (Ntsu)
Aquila wahlbergi (60 cm) (135)
The only brown eagle to breed in South Africa in summer; also a migrant bird, occuring singly or in pairs; fairly common and recognised by deep yellow cere, gape and legs.

Vultures (Manong)
Large, scavenging birds of prey; soar high on thermals, using excellent sight to find carcasses; cannot grip prey with talons, but use powerful beaks to tear carcasses open.

Cape Vulture (Lenong)
Gyps coprotheres (1,1 m) (122)
At one time, most common vulture in South Africa, but threatened by farmers as it has been known to attack sheep; nests communally on cliff ledges.

Lappetfaced Vulture
(Lenong) *Torgos tracheliotus* (1 m) (124)
Largest resident vulture; female larger than male; known to attack live prey.

Whitebacked Vulture (Lenong)
Gyps africanus (95 cm) (12
Similar to Cape vultur but smaller; normal outnumber other vultures; lay or egg May – Ju

Black Korhaan (Tlatlagwe)
Eupodotis afra (53 cm) (239)
Males very noisy, females shy; 1 - 2 eggs laid on ground Oct – Feb.

Kori Bustard (Kgori)
Ardeotis kori (1,3 m) (230)
Heaviest flying bird in the world, with males weighing up to 19 kg; only fly when threatened; usually occur alone, but may congregate in flocks of 30 or more; eat seed, carrion and small vertebrates; male inflates neck and fans tail over back to attract female.

Redcrested Korhaan (Tlatlagwe)
Eupodotis ruficrista (50 cm) (237)
Very fast fliers; red crest of male seldom seen; males have acrobatic courtship flight.

Couch Grass
Cynodon dactylon
(45 cm)

SPECIES GUIDE

Large Birds

Descended from reptiles, birds have survived on earth due to the special adaptation of flight. Although humans have mastered this secret, no man-made machine will ever match the magical flight of birds.

Pilanesberg boasts over 300 bird species. Some are migrants, others permanent inhabitants; some eat carrion or live prey; others eat seeds, fruit or tiny water organisms. And all of them are specifically adpated to their way of life. This page will help identify some of Pilanesberg's larger birds – the "Kings of the Sky"; whose flight has inspired people for centuries.

Secretarybird (Ramolongwana)
Sagittarius serpentarius (1,5 m) (118)
Terrestrial bird of prey; loose plume-like quills look like olden day secretaries' pens; walk proudly, stopping to shuffle feet in search of insects, rodents and reptiles; snakes are circled with widespread wings, trampled to death, then swallowed whole.

Ostrich (Ntshwe)
Struthio camelus (2 m) (1)
World's largest bird weighing up to 156 kg; can run up to 70 km/h; eat pebbles to assist digestion; male has a lion-like roar, often at night; male and female protect nest, sometimes giving fatal kicks to intruders.

Blue Buffalo Grass
Cenchrus ciliaris (1 m)

Experience a Different World

Death's Head Hawk Moth (Serurubele)
Acherontia atropos (110 mm)

Pearlspotted Owl (Morubitshi)
Glaucidium perlatum (18 cm) (398)
Smallest owl in southern Africa weighing 50 gm; has false eyes on back of head; active at dawn and dusk; often mobbed by other birds when resting; hunts insects, birds and bats; call is a repetitive ascending *'tee tee tee tee teeu teeu teeu'* then descending.

Looper Moth (Serurubele)
Xylopteryx protearia

Praying Mantis (Maseletswana)
Sphodromantis gastrica (85 mm)

Spotted Eagle Owl (Morubitshi)
Bubo africanus (47 cm) (401)
Most common owl in southern Africa; has slit ears behind the eyes; hunts rodents, small mammals, reptiles and birds; lays eggs under rocky overhangs, in hollow tree-stumps, or in other birds' nests; call is a typical hooting *'hu hoo'*.

Common Striped Skink
Mabuya striata striata (18 - 25 cm L)

Common Cricket (Senyetse)
Gryllus bimaculatus (28 mm)

Aardvark/Antbear (Thakadu)
Orycteropus afer (160 cm L, including tail)
Strong bear-like claws dig for ants and termites, then uses 30 cm, sticky tongue; excavated termite mounds become burrows for many other animals like hyaena, warthog and even bats and owls; solitary, has very poor eyesight but keen senses of smell and hearing; has scent glands between back legs.

Nightjars (Bomamauwane)
Family Caprimulgidae (23 - 28 cm) (404 - 408)
Well-camouflaged birds with long, pointed wings; fly silently as they hawk insects, especially beetles; roost and nest on the ground moving their eggs when they suspect detection.

Large-spotted Genet (Nakedi/Tshipa)
Genetta tigrina (100 cm L, including tail)
Black-tipped tail distinguishes it from small-spotted genet; each one has own unique body pattern; stalk prey in leopard fashion, catching insects, spiders, birds, reptiles and small rodents.

African Civet (Tsaparangaka)
Civettictis civetta (40 cm H)
Claws are doglike and non-retractable; territorial and solitary; dung contains seed, hair and exoskeletons of millipedes; secretion from anal glands was once used in perfumes.

Spotted Dikkop (Mmutlanakana)
Burhinus capensis (44 cm) (297)
Insectivorous; can be seen sleeping during the day in shade; run with head low when disturbed; calls a piping *'ti ti ti ti tee'* rising in pitch and volume, then dying down.

Porcupine (Noko)
Hystrix africaeaustralis (85 cm L)
Largest rodent in Africa; will walk backwards towards an intruder with vibrating quills raised, sometimes inflicting fatal wounds; can travel 20 km a night foraging for tubers, bulbs or roots; ring-barks trees and gnaws bones to sharpen incisors and obtain minerals.

NIGHT SPECIES

Experience a Different World

As night falls, stealth, secrecy and surprise spread across the African bush. Now, specialised and unusual species venture out from their daytime hiding, to take advantage of the darkness. Adaptations of sight have made animals like cats, owls, bats and bushbabies, successful nocturnal hunters.

The hunted, who lack this visual advantage, are alert to every sound and every smell. Night animals can also be seen around sunset, before darkness falls.
You may also be lucky to spot these nocturnal animals in the early dawn.

Lesser Bushbaby (Kgajwanamasigo)
Galago moholi (37 cm L, including tail)
Live in trees; forage alone for gum and insects but sleep in family groups in a platform nest with tail and hands covering huge eyes; wipe urine on their feet to scent-mark; make sounds like a baby crying; preyed on by genets and owls.

Aardwolf (Mmabudu/Mabudu)
Proteles cristatus (50 cm H)
Long mane often raised in excitement; long curved canines, other teeth reduced in size; eats up to 200 000 insects a night, mainly termites.

Brown Hyaena (Phiri)
Hyaena brunnea (80 cm H)
Long mane erected when alarmed, making it look fearsome; scavenger but also hunts small prey, using excellent sense of smell; white droppings characterised by high hair content; territorial males have large home-ranges, marked by scent paste from anal glands. (See Map, Point 43)

Caracal (Thwane)
Felis caracal (45 cm H)
Rare solitary animal; only eats fresh prey; males fiercely defend territories; kittens are helpless at birth and are well hidden.

Scrub Hare (Mmutla)
Lepus saxatilis (55 cm L)
Can often be seen darting ahead of cars at night; a grazer that eats its own dung pellets to obtain full nutrients; males fight viciously over females; unlike rabbits, baby hares can run soon after birth; their defence is to lie still with ears flattened; they also swim well; preyed on by many carnivores and large birds of prey.

HISTORY
Humans and Nature

Many people say that the Garden of Eden lay in Africa, a natural paradise where people and animals lived side by side. History was born here, and for millions and millions of years, man and animal co-existed, changing and surviving within the protection of the ancient volcano. Today, this is still so, and the story continues to unfold.

Early Stone Age

2,5 million years ago, our early ancestors invented the first tools – crude hand axes, choppers, irregular cutting flakes, and later, multi-purpose axes and cleavers. This development was as important then, as landing on the moon is to us now.

This period lasted for 2 million years. Early people depended solely on their environment and on their own growing intelligence. They gathered food or scavenged for it, but had not yet learned to hunt large game. Like many of the animals, they were the prey of predators like the sabre-toothed tiger (see illustration showing tiger tooth marks). But unlike other mammals, stone age people ran on two legs and had the use of their hands.

Middle Stone Age

Between 200 000 and 40 000 years ago a new age began – the spine of prehistoric man had straightened. We call these people Homo Sapiens. They had developed more advanced tools, like sharp stone points and flake blades. To increase their safety and comfort, they took shelter in caves and lit fires against the freezing cold. This period saw the last Ice Age cover the earth in frozen snows and glaciers.

By then, Homo Sapiens had become skilled hunters. The common hunting technique was to drive game into pit traps. There is evidence that by the end of this period a number of animal species had already been hunted into extinction by humans.

TOOLS AND WEAPONS OF TODAY AND YESTERDAY

Humans and Nature

Late Stone Age

This period occurred between 40 000 BC and 300 AD. It is associated with the San who were hunter-gatherers, and the Khoekhoe who were stock herders of cattle and goats. About 6 000 years ago the climate became much warmer, making survival easier. This was assisted by the development of new tools, like the scraper, and of course the bow and arrow. The San were very skilled hunters. With this new technology, they had time for leisure and time to think. They painted on rocks and made engravings, telling the stories of their lives and their religious beliefs. There are some fine examples of rock art in the Park, but they are well off the beaten track.

Early Iron Age

In about 300 AD, huge changes swept the sub-continent. Bantu speaking people arrived from the north with new ways and a new technology. This transformed the area forever. They brought crops and the knowledge of iron. They also smelted copper and gold, made pottery and kept domestic stock. A new concept was born – the acquisition of wealth.

For the first time, humans took more than just their basic needs from nature, and this placed significant stress on the environment. Iron smelting needed charcoal and there was plenty of this to be found in the dense woodlands and forests. In addition, bush had to be cleared to make way for crops like cow-peas, sorghum, millet and ground beans. Society revolved around keeping goats and cattle, and villages were built around the animal kraals. To enter the village, visitors would first walk through the kraal to see the wealth and strength of the chief and his people. Basic survival was now softened by the security of wealth.

Remains of skeletons and graves in the area show that ochre, symbolical of blood, was used for burials. This ritual was possibly one of the first religious sparks in human history.

The San lived a nomadic existence, following game and rainfall across the vast African plains. Rain meant life. Drought often meant death. Rain gods were invoked through trance dances. Similar rituals were later practiced by Tswana people who built shrines to the rain god. Such shrines have been found in Pilanesberg.

Climatically, this period was one of see-sawing change. From 100-200 AD it was colder than it is today, but it warmed up again between 200-600 AD. Then again, a much colder period took over between 600-900 AD. These changes affected the movement of people. They settled when conditions were good and moved away when it was too dry or too cold.

Despite their greater security, people were still dependent on nature. They moved with the changes of climate and season, and with the movement of game. They still obeyed nature's laws, but they had learned to use it to their advantage.

HISTORY
Humans and Nature
(continued)

Late Iron Age

Between 1000 AD and the 1830's, the population in the North West area increased significantly. Inevitable conflict lay ahead. The first half of this millenium was characterised by settlements on foothills of mountains. From about 1600 AD, large stone structures were built on the tops of hills, from where enemies could be seen easily, and the village better defended. Huge 'mega-sites' (1 - 3 kilometres across), housing up to 20 000 people, sprung up on large, open areas in the North West. Such a site can be seen at Malokwane, south-west of the Pilanesberg. Within Pilanesberg however, smaller sites were built on foothills. From here a village had good views, but at the same time, was well hidden from enemies. There were no 'mega-sites' in Pilanesberg. This meant less stress on the environment.

Between 1400 and 1850, climatic changes occurred once again – a cold, dry period (the Little Ice Age) was followed by warmer, wetter conditions. Around 1800, flooding rains and much higher temperatures brought prosperity to the land and people.

With more and more people entering the area that is now the North West, it was not long before competition for resources shattered the peace.

The late 18th and early 19th century was a time of great turbulence and violence. Sometimes known as the Mfecane, or the 'scattering', this time saw many chiefdoms and people move around within South Africa. New chiefdoms moved into the North West area.

The Bakgatla

Between 1700 and 1750, the Bakgatla people established themselves near present-day Saulspoort (at the northern tip of the Park). They belonged to the Tswana linguistic group. Under the leadership of Chief Masselane, they trekked from Hammanskraal, near present day Pretoria. But the new pastures were ruled by the Batlhako tribe, and for a while the Bakgatla had to pay tribute to live there. When they refused to continue payment, war broke out. The Bakgatla won and enjoyed some years of dominance in the area.

Pilanesberg is named after the Bakgatla chief, Pilane, who ruled between 1825 and 1850.

No one could have risen to power at a more difficult time, because in 1825, the Ndebele warlord, Mzilikaze, swept into the region. He brought turbulence and terror, subduing Pilane's people, imposing taxes and forcing them to look after his cattle. Mzilikaze's war parties caused havoc throughout the North West. With so many corpses littering the bushveld, lions developed a taste for human flesh. People built their huts on platforms or in trees to be safe from these marauding lions.

PILANESBERG'S HISTORICAL TIME-LINE
1 mm = 2 000 years

EARLY STONE AGE 2 500 000 - 200 000 BC

Humans and Nature

By the end of the 1800's, European settlers had established themselves permanently and had assumed control in the region. Indigenous people could not dispute the power of guns and horses and were quickly subdued.

Then a new force, the army of the British Empire, arrived to challenge the power of the Boers. Although the second Boer War (1899-1902), did not directly affect the Pilanesberg, the whole region was influenced economically, politically and environmentally.

Europeans continued to rule the land for almost another century.

Arrival of Settlers from Europe

Around this time missionaries and European settlers began to move into the area. Mzilikaze did not tolerate their presence, except for one extraordinary case. To this day, it remains a fascinating story – the missionary, Robert Moffat entered the region in 1829. He and the Ndebele warlord struck up an instant friendship. Other trespassers were violently chased out but Mzilikaze regarded Moffat as a friend, and even a brother.

Mzilikaze's reign of terror lasted until a combined force of Tswana, Griqua and European settlers drove him out. This was not the first, or last time, that black and white settlers joined to oust a common enemy. The Ndebele fled to southern Zimbabwe and established themselves in Bulawayo.

In 1863 the Dutch Reformed Church established a mission station at Saulspoort. The Bakgatla chief, Kgamanyane, Pilane's son, converted to Christianity. Even today, most Bakgatla are still members of the church. However they have retained many of the old traditions, and still have the same totem animal, the vervet monkey.

They also still practice the old Tswana initiation rites. Known as *bogwera*, this teaches the laws and marriage customs of the people as well as knowledge of the environment. It usually takes place in winter and can last 2 - 3 weeks. Young men must bathe in a cold stream and undergo circumcision, before entering adulthood.

Further Influences

Over this last century, cycles of conflict and resolution, and the rapid advance in technology, have left their mark on the Pilanesberg. The most dramatic effect on the environment came from mechanised agriculture, large herds of domestic stock, and huge hunting expeditions. This saw the gradual disappearance of wild animals, and the temporary destruction of natural habitats.

Smaller influences on the environment had always occurred. For instance Iron Age communities planted *Euphorbia* trees around their homes. These were regarded as magical and medicinal trees, and can still be seen at old village sites in the Park.

A direct influence of nature on man came from the surface water in Pilanesberg. Volcanic rock formations here contain large amounts of fluoride. This is taken up in the water and causes the teeth of long-term inhabitants in the area to go brown (dental fluorosis). At one time, it was said that they could not believe the pure white teeth of newcomers to the area. Today water is piped in from other sources.

The most dramatic influence that man and nature have had on each other in the Pilanesberg, happened very recently. For the first time in the area, people came to assist nature, and not only use it for their own benefit.

In 1979 the Pilanesberg Park was born...

PRESENT DAY
LATE IRON AGE 1000 AD - 1830
EARLY IRON AGE 300 - 1000 AD
LATE STONE AGE 40 000 BC - 300 AD
MIDDLE STONE AGE 200 000 - 40 000 BC

PILANESBERG PARK
Creation and Conservation

Creating the Pilanesberg Park has been a long and complicated process. Since its birth in 1979, dedicated people have nurtured and nourished it. Today it still requires huge effort, careful planning and a vision of the future.

By the year 2 000 AD, some 80 million eco-tourists, worldwide, will visit places like Pilanesberg every year. As more and more of us enjoy the outdoors, we have to ask – can nature sustain itself, as well as us? And how can we give it a helping hand?

These pages show that Pilanesberg is a managed system, involving veld, animal and people management. This is the way to ensure future generations will also benefit from our natural heritage.

Park History

Pilanesberg Park was first conceived in 1969. It took ten years of research and legislation before it finally opened on 8 December 1979. But before it could be stocked with game, the 55 000 hectare area had to be prepared.

The first step was to remove all evidence of mechanised farming and mining. Houses, fences, windmills, pumps and mining equipment were dismantled and trucked away. Tons of alien vegetation were removed and indigenous vegetation was seeded in its place. The battle to reclaim eroded land began. Eventually, the area was fenced and Operation Genesis began.

Generously funded by the South African Nature Foundation, and many other organisations, this operation remains the largest game translocation in the world. 5 957 animals of 19 different species were initially moved in from parks across southern Africa. Even the fabled Noah did not have to contend with 50 elephants, 1937 impala, or 19 critically endangered black rhino, to mention a few. Due to veterinary restrictions, most animals were quarantined in a 1 200 hectare boma, before final release.

Translocating animals to and from Pilanesberg continues. So does the management of these animals and the habitats in which they live.

In addition, management must take care of approximately 120 000 visitors a year...

Creation and Conservation

Veld Management

Conserving habitat is of vital importance. Without their habitats, no animals would survive. A few aspects of veld management are outlined here.

- Erosion is controlled by building rock packs, gabions, contour drains, dams and weirs. This prevents valuable soil being washed away.
- Most of Pilanesberg is covered in unpalatable sourveld. Veld burning is necessary as it encourages palatable grass to grow.
- Alien plants which are poisonous to game and destructive to natural habitats, are always being removed.
- Good veld management is the basis of good animal management.

People Management

Large numbers of visitors could have a negative impact on the Park. But revenue from tourism also keeps the Park alive. A delicate balance is therefore needed between people and the Pilanesberg. Looking after visitors includes the building and maintainance of roads, hides, picnic and view sites. This is an ongoing task aimed at making your visit more enjoyable.

Law enforcement is very important. Respecting the Park's laws allows management to get on with looking after the animals and their habitats.

Animal Management

Today it is said that animals must 'pay their way' if they are to survive in such a full and competitive world. Wildlife must benefit people, and people must benefit wildlife. Here are a few points that help to ensure this:

- Excess game is translocated to other parks. In 1994, Pilanesberg sold 19 white rhino for R361 000. This money benefits the Park and the people living around it.
- A game census is conducted every year. If there are too many animals, some must be culled. This prevents the destruction of habitats.
- Veterinary control prevents disease. Constant research and monitoring of animals helps keep a sustainable natural balance in the Park.
- Scout patrols guard against poachers and check that fences are intact.

Looking after our natural heritage is a 24 hour a day job for the Park's management team. But it is important to realise that by being here, and obeying the laws, you too are making a positive difference.

Thank you for keeping Pilanesberg beautiful.

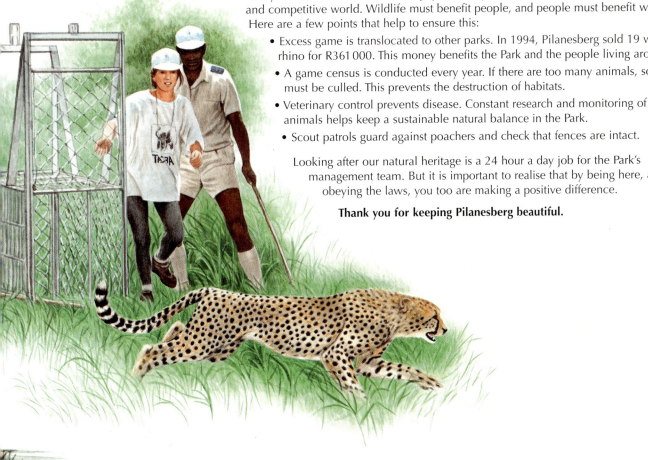

STORIES TOLD BY THE OLD MAN OF MORULENG

Pilanesberg is a unique area where,
after massive volcanic upheavals,
a natural sanctuary was created within rings of mountains.
For thousands of years animals, man and plants have lived
here relying on one another, or fighting each other, for
food, shelter and homes for their young.

Discovering Pilanesberg can be more than just
a glimpse of one, two or (if you are lucky),
three of the Big Five.

The following pages are designed to help you enjoy
your visit to the maximum, and to give you an
understanding of the rules of the Park.

The rules are there to keep you safe
– the Big Five are not given that name lightly!
There are also rules to keep Pilanesberg as beautiful,
peaceful and unspoilt as it is now.

Stories told by
the Old Man of Moruleng
(Pages 45-47)

These stories highlight cultural information from
the Bakgatla and Bakubung people.
(See pages 40 and 45-47.)

Pilanesberg Map
(Pages 48-49)

This Map will help you plan your trip,
and guide you as you travel.
It also gives you distances, a summary of facilities,
and the numbers for the Points of Discovery.

Points of Discovery
(Pages 50-57)

From the fascinating world of insects, to magical and
medicinal trees, these Discovery Points will provide
the clues as to where… and why…
and how it all happens in Pilanesberg.

One day I was sitting at **Moruleng, the Place of the Marulas,** eating the juicy fruits, when an Old, Old Man came to me. He sat down. He did not speak for a very long time but sat quietly, listening, and watching the bush. Much later, by the fire, he began to speak, and his voice glowed like the setting sun.

Stories told by the old man

"You, know, it is good to enjoy the peace and quiet of this place. When I was a boy I learned many secrets from the bush because I was always quiet and patient. Not like **Mokoe the Grey Lourie** whose noisy call says '*go away*'. Some local people believe that even if you imitate the call of Makoe, your lips will dry up and crack?" With this the Old Man smiled.

Mokoe, see page 23

"You know", the Old Man said, "I myself remember the stories my grandfather told. He, like me, was of the **Bakgatla Tribe, the People of the Monkey.** It is our totem animal, and it is honoured and respected by the people of the Pilanesberg. We believe, to eat the flesh of the monkey will make the gods very angry and they will blow the roof off your house."

Kgabo, see page 18

"**The Bakubung Tribe, the People of the Hippo,** believe the same of the hippo. It is their totem. Long ago people believed this was the truth. Today it is more like a story for most of us, but it is an important part of our culture.
And we still respect all animals, and all cultures."

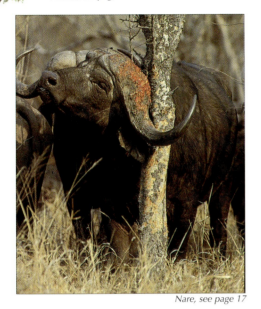

Nare, see page 17

"It can be dangerous, especially if **Tlou the Elephant, Tau the Lion, Tshukudu the Rhino and Nare the Buffalo** are around. In Setswana we say '*e re o gopola tshukudu o ikanye sethlare*', meaning if you even think of a rhino, you must hide away. In English we say '*speak of the Devil and he will appear*'."

"There are many wonderful stories in the bush", he continued. "They have been told to each generation for thousands and thousands of years. Some of it is wisdom, some of it may just be stories … Do you know old Rapula? Well, he had problems with his wife and they could not have children, so the Traditional Healer told him to eat the bark of **Morokolo the Num-num Tree**. Well, after that, they had many, many children." Again, the Old Man smiled, his eyes twinkling with humour and wisdom. "Yes, the bush has great magic, but if you destroy it, disturb, or spoil it, you will never see the magic or the power, or the beauty of nature."

Morokolo, see page 20

Tau, see page 15

Nowadays all animals are protected.

Here in Pilanesberg we are their guests, in their home.

"Now **Nkwe the Leopard** is a difficult animal to see and photograph. But we often see his tracks all over the Park, especially at **Mankwe, the Place of the Leopard.** You know that it is a sacred animal for our people. Killing a leopard was a crime punishable by death. The only one allowed to wear the skin was **Kgosi the Chief.**"

Stories told by the old man

It is important not to feed any of the animals or birds. They all know how to feed themselves best.

"If you go fast you won't see much game. The animals' camouflage will deceive your eyes. And by driving off-road you might destroy someone's home, or drive over their young. Small creatures, like children, are all important in the chain of life."

Korwe, see page 20

"Talking of children, some people used to call my father **Korwe, the Hornbill,** because he was like this bird, who will go hungry as long as his chicks are well fed. Animals, like humans, protect their young."

"Now here is an interesting story about **Tshukudu the Rhino** and children. Did you know the white rhino calf always walks in front of the mother? We say '*Tshukudu kwa gobe e isiwa ke ngwana.*' This means '*that children always lead their parents into trouble.*'" With this the Old Man burst into laughter.

"Here is another story about children and **Legodi the Glossy Starling**. It is said that if a spoilt child wants this bird, you must give it to him, because the bird will peck the child and teach it a lesson."

Legodi, see page 20

"You know to learn nature's many secrets we must just watch and try to change it as little as possible. We have threatened so many animals already. This is why we do not feed the animals. By doing so we create dependency. After a while animals cannot feed themselves, they starve, or have to be shot by rangers – especially **Tshwene the Baboon**."

Throughout the book Setswana names of the species have been added where possible.

Tshwene, see page 25

"One animal that most people believe is very dangerous is **Noga the Snake**. But snakes are good. They control pests like rodents. Local people say if you see Noga, you must stand with one foot on top of the other to keep yourself from running away. If you are dead still, snakes will leave you alone. **But it is always best to be careful when walking.**"

"Another reptile is **Gopane the Monitor Lizard**. It is believed that if you kill it, it will bring on a storm, but if you turn it around, it will stop the wind. An old story goes that this lizard sucks milk from the goat by winding its tail around the goat's legs and then milking it until it actually starts to bleed.

Can you imagine? It is good to imagine!"

Gopane, see page 26

Pitse e Tilodi, see page 13 & Thutlwa, see page 21

Stories told by the old man

"**M**yth, magic and healing are all part of our local culture. Many people laugh, but today they are learning to see the value in the old stories and to use plants more and more. Plants are great healers you know. We talked of magic before – now many trees have magical powers too, and many myths surround them."

"**O**ld people with great wisdom believe that to cut **Morula the Marula Tree** in winter, will bring on storms. We use the tree to help cure colds, diarrhoea, dysentery and to make delicious jelly and beer. The marula is like a natural restaurant for man and animals in Africa."

"**M**osetlha the Weeping Wattle is also said to have magical powers. If one of a couple dies, the survivor must drink wattle bark to cleanse the blood of the dead person. If both people die, we say '*Baile – they are gone*'."

Morula, see page 17

Mosetlha, see page 14

"**Z**ulu people say the thorns of **Mokgalo the Buffalo Thorn** will wipe out a dead person's spirit and bury it. It is believed that Mokgalo is home to their ancestors. And the tree is used as a pain killer; also to treat infections, dysentery, lumbago and chest complaints; and as a protection against lightning."

Trees are great healers and we must look after them.

"**U**nmanaged fires destroy these important plants. Today, because of fences, animals cannot escape if there is a fire. Do you know there is a bird that is said to bring fire? Some say that if **Letlekere the Lilacbreasted Roller** perches on your tree or house, it brings bad luck and 'invites' lightning and fire."

"**M**orubitshi the Owl is another bird traditionally associated with bad luck. They say it can 'invite' witches to your house. Many cultures all over the world believe this about Morubitshi. But owls are really good as they eat rodents and other pests. We also say about owls, '*Morubitshi ga o bonwe, o bonwe ke Motsoga pele*', which means only early risers see unusual things. And the best time for discovery in Pilanesberg is early morning or late afternoon."

"**N**ow **Pupupu the African Hoopoe** we believe brings good luck. Look for these birds! Maybe they will tell you something in your dreams. What some people call superstition, other people may call belief, religion, psychology or culture. It is important to realize the value of culture. Culture gives people identity and uniqueness. And African culture is one of the oldest in the world."

We are happy to share this great richness with you.

Nkwe, see page 14

"**I**t is no laughing matter to run out of water, or to be stuck in the bush overnight. I know. Once when Pilanesberg was still farmland, I followed a lost cow way past **Dithabaneng, the Place of the Small Hills**, and I got lost. That night I heard **Nkwe the Leopard** coughing. I did not sleep much in that uncomfortable tree! And the next day I was so thirsty. Luckily…"

By now it was dark and the Old Man continued to tell stories about our animals long into the night. He spoke about them as if they were his friends and I know that, yes, they were his friends.

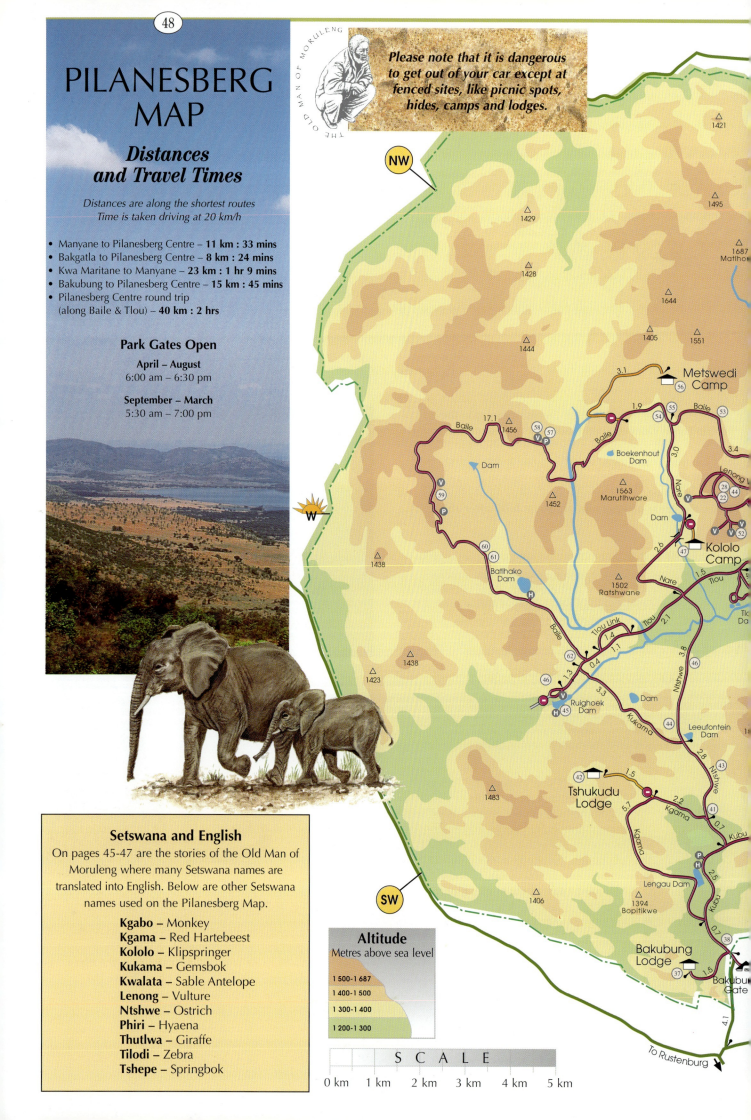

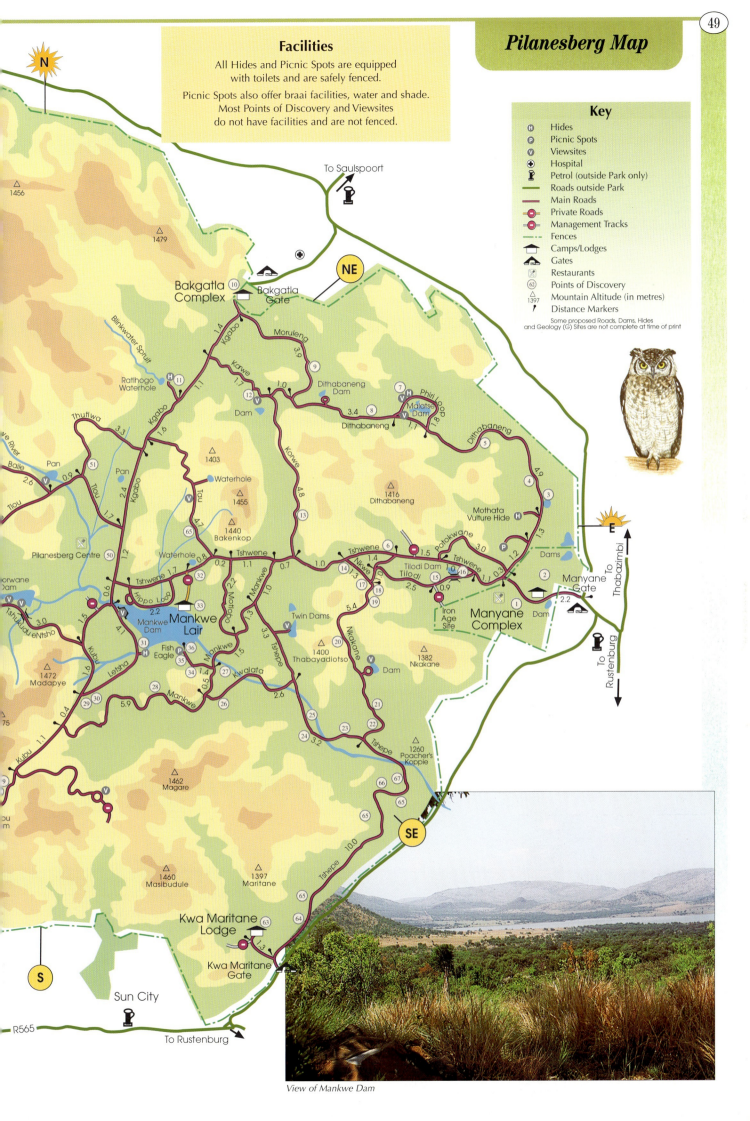

POINTS OF DISCOVERY

2 Walking Area
(Self-guided trails)
Stretch your legs and enjoy nature at close range, by experiencing the Walking Area at Manyane. This area is fenced and has no large, dangerous animals. A route map and guide to interesting features is available. This offers environmental education while enjoying game viewing or bird watching on foot.

Tilodi, see page 13

3 Salty Spring
A mineral hotspot that provides animals with vital nutrients all year long.

4 Shepherd's Tree Area
The unusual *Boscia foetida* or 'Stinkwitgat' is drought resistant. It gets its name from the pungent smell of the flowers and inner wood. The edible fruit tastes like capers.

Motlopi, see page 21

5 Volcanic Tuff G1
1 300 million years ago a volcanic eruption blasted massive rocks, kilometers into the sky. The biggest boulders fell back to earth first; smaller ones scattered at random above them. A series of blasts, over time, created layers of these rocks, called tuffs. Erosion has exposed them to us.

Please Note as you drive through the Park:
- The Discovery Points are not necessarily in numerical order.
- Some numbers are repeated at more than one place in the Park.
- Not all points are right next to the road. Look around carefully where the point is marked.
- Geological sites (G1-15) are indicated with their relevant rock colours on these pages.

6 Management Sites
Throughout the Park you can see efforts to curb erosion, help rehabilitate over-used areas and create attractive sites. Silt traps, weirs, dams, gabions and rock packs are some examples of management control (see page 43).

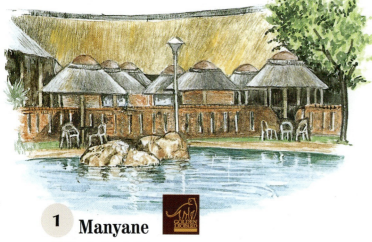

1 Manyane
- Self-catering chalets
- Conference facilities (up to 88 people)
- Caravan park with 100 fully-electrified caravan stands, 60 camping sites, ablution & laundry facilities
- A lá carte restaurant, shop & bar
- Swimming pool, jungle gym, mini-golf (putt-putt).
- Walk-in aviary (over 80 species of indigenous birds)
- Bosele Camp with dormitories; fully catered (for school groups up to 204 children)

Contact: Tel: (01465) 56135
Fax: (01465) 57555

*Leave only your tracks.
Take only your photographs.
Please do not litter
or pick anything.*

Points of discovery

7 Malatse Hide (Fenced)
A site showing management's efforts to restore nature and to provide visitors with rewarding viewing. The weir and man-made dam prevent erosion and have encouraged wildlife back to this dry part of the Park. Sable, eland and rhino may be among the rewards for patient viewers.

8 Nepheline Syenite G2
This rock was formed when boiling magma rose to just below the earth's surface. Here it cooled down rapidly and solidified. White feldspar crystals were captured in the direction of the flowing magma.

9 Gully Thickets
Remnants of ancient forests survive where two hillsides meet. These gullies collect water and soil, and the denser vegetation provides good habitat for leopard, bushbuck, kudu and a wealth of forest birds.

10 Bakgatla
- Manyane style brick chalets set in attractive mountains
- Full facilities & swimming pool
- Braai & picnic sites with kiosk, ablutions & children's playground

Contact: Tel: (01465) 56135
Fax: (01465) 57555

Kolobe ya Naga, see page 33

11 Ratlhogo Hide (Fenced)
An excellent hide to watch game coming down to drink, mud-rollers (like warthog) enjoying a wallow, terrapin and birds. The karree trees are indicative of wet areas. Thick bush provides good cover for kudu, bushbuck, waterbuck and other woodland species.

12 Lava G3
As lava flowed on the earth's surface, it cooled rapidly through exposure to air and wind.

13 Soil Formation
Large boulders tumble down from the hills, eventually crumbling into soil. The ongoing process of soil formation takes thousands of years. This process is easy to see in hundreds of places in Pilanesberg.

14 Kimberlite G4
In the 1920's a fortune-seeking prospector discovered this Kimberlite pipe. The bright red garnets he found here could have indicated diamonds; so he dug in excitement, but in vain!

15 Tamboti Circle
You can recognise Tamboti by their dark, blocky bark. Black Rhino and porcupine enjoy these highly poisonous trees, but smoke of burning wood causes nausea and headaches in humans. In Nov-Jan look out for tamboti 'jumping beans' – the catterpillars of a small grey moth spasmodically stretching inside the Tamboti seeds.

Morukuru, see page 30

16 Masked Weaver Colony
Weavers flock to this water habitat for safety and food. Man-made dams often create new habitats for many species.

Thaga, see page 31

Morula, see page 17

17 Marula Area
The magic Marula means food, drink, medicine and myth in Africa. It is traditionally used to treat colds, dysentery, diarrhoea, and as an anti-hystamine; also to increase fertility in women.

Moumo, see page 24

18 Rock Figs
Some *Ficus* species take root in rocks, splitting them with their geotropic (earth-seeking) force. Their white roots are distinctive on many rocky areas throughout the Park.

Points of discovery

We must be careful not to start fires – never throw cigarettes or matches into the veld.

— THE OLD MAN OF MORULENG

19 Live-long Tree
The *Lannea discolor* is said to cure fever and constipation. Poles, fishing floats and twine are made from it.

Mmotshwana, see page 12

20 Uranium-bearing Rock
This rock is a continuation of G13 (Point 25) on the other side of the hill. Such 'spurs' can go on for miles underground, being exposed through erosion at some points.

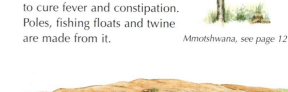

21 Flat Rock and Natural Seep
A natural seep causes permanent water to collect and attracts game to this area.

22 Resurrection Plant
A hardy plant that appears dead in dry times, but a little water brings it to miraculous life.

23 Termite Mounds
This old farm area has been colonised by termites. This is the first step to rehabilitation, as termites eat the dead wood from felled trees, and soon birds and game return to lengthen the food chain.

Moswiarula, see page 25

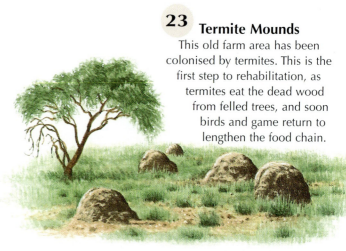

24 Black Eagle Valley
A pair of black eagles breed 2 km up the valley. Black eagles pair for life and can be seen in flight or perched on rocks.

Ntsu, see page 27

25 Uranium-bearing Tuff G13
These tuffs (see Point 5) are mildly radioactive due to their uranium content. The minerals in these rocks are a result of super-heated water (200-400°C) which soaked into the rock at the end of the volcanoes' active life.

26 Black Thorn Area
Indicative of nutritious sweetveld, these *Acacia mellifera* trees are excellent fodder for browsers. Grass is sometimes lacking in sweetveld, as it is well utilized by grazers. In old times, these trees were used to form kraals or to snare fish driven down a narrow stream.

27 Fish Eagle Nest
For many years this has been home to a pair of fish eagles. Like the black eagle, these birds mate for life. They live in a fiercely defended territory and often return to the same nest for generations. Look in the wooded area, quite far off the road.

Mongana, see page 22

Kgoadira, see page 30

Points of discovery

28 Transvaal Beech
These fire-resistant trees are indicative of Sourveld which does not provide much nutrition in winter. Due to the accumulation of dry, unpalatable grasses, Sourveld burns very easily. A red dye is made from these *Faurea saligna* trees.

Mofufu, see page 23

29 Red Syenite G7
This makes good polished facing stone. Twenty years ago attempts to quarry it failed as it contains small, yellow grains of iron oxide which do not polish well. On the hill behind this site, long, vertical, drilling holes can be seen (see Point 67).

30 Red Balloon Tree
An extremely rare plant occuring only in syenite koppies. It can be seen above the drilled rocks at G7 (Point 29), growing almost out of the rock. This tree is protected in South Africa.

31 Mankwe Lake View Platform (Fenced)
Situated in the centre of Pilanesberg, this spot offers excellent viewing, especially of waterbirds. The domed hills bear testament to volcanic activity, pushed out through plugs in the earth's crust. Crocodile and hippo rule the water and birds come to breed and feed nearby.

32 White Foyaite G5
The surrounding hills are white foyaite, a coarse-grained rock that crystallised slowly from molten magma inside the earth. It is rich in minerals, like feldspar and nepheline and the rare metal, zirconium (see Points 35 and 38).

33 Mankwe
- Camp overlooks Mankwe Lake
- 10 rustic, self-catering, safari-style tents & 10 single-room wooden cabins (bedding provided)
- Paraffin lamps, flush toilets & reed-walled showers
- Central kitchen with fridge

Contact: Tel: (01465) 56135
Fax: (01465) 57555

34 Common Tree Euphorbia
A cactus-like plant, the *Euphorbia ingens*, is enjoyed by Black Rhino. The San used it to make poison arrows and its milky latex can blind people. Some say the tree is a protection against lightning. They are often home to genets and bushbabies.

Ngoge, see page 24

35 White Foyaite G14
Foyaites are not easily weathered. This explains why the hills in this area are prominent (see Points 32 and 38).

36 Fish Eagle Picnic Site (Fenced)
The superb view, variety of trees, distinctive rocks and the interface of three habitats (rocky outcrop, hillside and water) make this attractive area a haven for wildlife. It was once a kraal site, being easily defendable and close to water. Trees include *Acacias*, bushwillows, Tamboti and Marula.

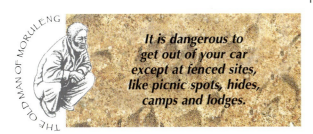

It is dangerous to get out of your car except at fenced sites, like picnic spots, hides, camps and lodges.

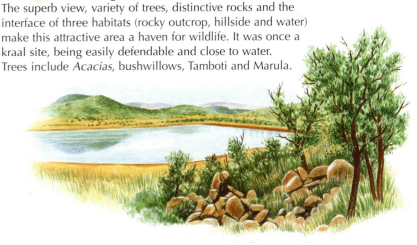

Points of discovery

Never get too close to animals. Do not tease them by throwing things, hooting or revving car engines.

THE OLD MAN OF MORULENG

37 Bakubung

- Superb hotel accommodation overlooking private dam with resident hippos
- Guided bush trails
- Bar area, restaurant, curio shop, conference centre & sporting facilities
- Afternoon, sunrise & sundowner game drives & bush braais

Contact: Tel: (01465) 21861
Fax: (01465) 21621

38 Green Foyaite G10
There are several varieties of foyaite with similar compositions, but differing proportions of minerals. The nepheline in this rock dissolves easily resulting in a pitted surface typical of the foyaites (see Point 53).

39 Wagon Tracks
From a century ago these tracks have left their mark in the oukliprock. Ouklip is formed when water evaporates leaving minerals behind. On the other side of the road on the far slope, are lines of trees – evidence of an old orchard. Indigenous trees have taken advantage of the old orchard holes.

40 Old Fluorite Mine G8
The old Moepo mine can be seen up against the mountain, where purple fluorite, containing calcium and fluorine, was mined. These minerals soaked into the rocks in the same way that mineralisation happened at Point 25.

41 Browser and Bird Area
Stop, look, listen and smell. Often a rewarding area for birds and browsers who come to thicket areas for food and safety (see pages 18 - 23).

42 TSHUKUDU

- 6 luxury thatched chalets, nestled against an isolated koppie and overlooking its own waterhole with superb game viewing
- Five star standards
- Game drives and walks accompanied by a ranger

Contact: Tel: (01465) 21610
Fax: (01465) 21620

43 Brown Hyaena Area
These shy, nocturnal animals are seldom seen, but keep a sharp lookout, especially on a night drive, because their lair is hidden nearby in the safety of the rocky hillsides. White middens may often be seen next to the road.

44 Sugarbush
The so-called sugarbush *(Protea caffra)* was depicted on the old South African 3 and 6 penny coins. Flowers Nov-Feb.

Phiri, see page 37

Points of discovery

45 Ruighoek Dam
A natural catchment area, surrounded by 4 prominent habitats – water, hillside, grassland and woodland. As a result many species occur, especially those dependent on water. A wide variety of trees including Karree, Wild Olive, Shepherd's Tree and Buffalo-thorn make this an excellent area for birds and game.

Nare, see page 17

46 Buffalo Area
Pilanesberg buffalo were introduced from Addo Elephant National Park as they were free of foot and mouth, and Corridor disease. To keep the herds healthy, buffalo from other regions will not be introduced. Look out for them in these areas.

47 Kololo
- 4 safari tents that sleep 3 people each (bedding provided)
- Located on a hilltop, overlooking wide open valley
- Central boma
- Only basic facilities provided

Contact:
Tel: (01465) 56135
Fax: (01465) 57555

48 Geographic Centre G15
This is the approximate geographic centre of the volcano. There are multiple, parallel bands of syenite and red foyaite, created over a million years ago from magma. This site is underwater for many months of the year.

49 Makorwane Dam (Fenced)
Another diversity of habitat with grassland, hills, rocky outcrops and water. Primary grassland and sweet thorn trees are the first stage of indigenous vegetation re-establishing on old farmlands. Note aloes on the hill and flooded trees which are good nesting sites. Dams help to recreate well-balanced water habitats.

50 Pilanesberg Centre
Built in 1936 as a Magistrate's Court, the Pilanesberg Centre has been converted into a restaurant and curio shop. Enjoy breakfast, lunch or tea from the terrace of this finely preserved building.

51 Graveyard
This graveyard dates back to the 1930's and is still visited by descendants of the family. It is Park policy not to remove old graves.

Animals have the right of way, so please do not exceed 40 km/h and keep on the road.

Points of discovery

52 Lenong View
Named after the vulture, this panoramic view sheds light on the Pilanesberg volcano. The mountains were once boiling magma, pushed up through concentric cracks in the earth's crust. These are called ring dykes, exposed to us through weathering. Scars of old farmland are evident in erosion and open, recovering grassland. Natural processes, assisted by management, rehabilitate the area. The mountain top is Sourveld where Transvaal Beech, Resurrection Plant, Sugarbush and Rock Figs grow. Eland, Mountain Reedbuck and Gemsbok can be found here.

53 Green Foyaite G6
In the surging sea of magma, deep below the earths' surface, many minerals were carried upwards. As the magma cooled they became set into rock. One of them is aegerine, which grew in a needle-like form in this green foyaite (see Point 38).

54 Reedbuck Area
Rewarding to see as they are shy and rare, Common Reedbuck are dependent on water and can be seen at vleis. Look out for Mountain Reedbuck on these hills.

Motlobo, see page 28

55 Driefontein
Once intensively farmed, the primary grassland has now returned and with it, the game. The exotic Belambra trees *(Phytolacca)* are not invasive and are enjoyed by elephants and other browsers. Most other exotics, like gum trees, have been removed by management.

56 Metswedi
- Luxurious safari-style tents with full catering, hot showers & baths
- Lounge/dining room area overlooking waterhole

Contact: Tel: (01465) 56135
Fax: (01465) 57555

57 Baile Picnic Spot (Fenced)
Mountains and rocky outcrops are home to baboon, klipspringer, leopard and large raptors. Good grassland nearby is where buffalo, reedbuck, giraffe and lion can be seen. This interface of two habitats draws a wide variety of species, especially birds.

58 Red Foyaite G9
The rugged country in this area is underlain by white foyaite. The red foyaite was created when super-heated water altered the composition and colour of the rock, through soaking it with red iron oxide.

Points of discovery

59 Baile Plain
A spectacular view of grasslands, rocky outcrops, hillsides, water and woodlands. Animals like White Rhino, wildebeest, springbok, zebra, and cheetah can be seen on the plain. A wide variety of trees germinate and seed easily in rocky areas where water and soil collect.

60 Rhino Rubbing Post
Some posts in the Park are smooth from years of White Rhino enjoying a good rub to remove parasites from their skin.

61 Church Site
This is a Dutch Reformed Church site, dating from 1964. The Wild Olive trees on this site were used to treat colic, sore eyes and throats. Also here are the large and beautiful White Stinkwood and the Buffalo-thorn, a sacred tree to the Zulu people.

62 White Rhino Middens
White rhino use this site as a territorial marker. Having stepped in the dung, the rhino walks his territory, ensuring it is well scented. Dung Beetles frequent the middens, laying eggs in the dung balls. The hatched grubs are eaten by birds, baboons, genets and civets, creating a long food chain in nature.

63 Kwa Maritane — Place of the Rock

STOCKS HOTELS AND RESORTS

- Luxurious hotel & timeshare game lodge, 5 bed luxury duplex cabanas or 8 bed chalets with private patios
- Conference centre, bar & restaurant overlooking illuminated waterhole
- Underground viewing hide
- Two swimming pools; tennis and volleyball courts
- Day and night game drives; bush braais

Contact:
Tel: (01465) 21820
Fax: (01465) 21268

64 Ledig Foyaite G11
This contains small, unharmful amounts of uranium, as well as aegerine (magnesium, iron, sodium and silica). It is also formed from magma.

65 Iron Age Walling
Walls can be seen throughout Pilanesberg. They date back to the 17th Century when Batswana settlements sprung up throughout the North West. Small villages were built at the base of hills so that look-outs could be easily posted without enemies detecting the village. Some may even have belonged to the infamous Matabele chief, Mzilikaze.

66 Klipspringer Koppie
This is a favoured area for this unusual antelope whose sure-footed hooves can cling to steep rock. The klipspringer, found throughout Africa, can live independently of water.

67 Red Syenite G12
Different from the syenite at 29, this is largely composed of potassium-rich orthoclase, feldspar, chlorite (iron, magnesium, silica and water), calcium and fluorine. Syenite is igneous rock, which means it formed from magma.

Kololo, see page 24

SPECIES TICK LIST

The following grids are for you to tick off your discoveries of plants, birds, mammals, reptiles and insects.

These have been set out with four columns so that you can keep separate counts on different days… or in different seasons… or on different trips…

Enjoy the discovery of finding it in Pilanesberg!

GRASSES

Page No.	TREES				
13	Aloe, Mountain				
28	Bean, Sumach				
23	Beech, Transvaal				
22	Black Thorn				
19	Buffalo Thorn				
12	Bushwillow, Large-fruited				
12	Red				
28	River				
12	Velvet				
24	Cabbage Tree				
24	Euphorbia, Common Tree				
26	Fever-berry, Lavender				
24	Fig, Large-leaved Rock				
18	Jacket-plum				
28	Karree				
14	Leadwood				
12	Live-long				
17	Marula				
18	Olive, Wild				
26	Pear, Common Wild				
21	Stink Shepherd's Tree				
16	Sweet Thorn				
30	Tamboti				
16	Umbrella Thorn				
14	Wattle, Weeping				

Page No.	SHRUBS				
32	Black-jack				
26	Fern, Hard				
32	Khaki Weed				
27	Lichen				
26	Mother-in-law's Tongue				
33	Nightshade				
20	Num-num				
22	Puzzle Bush				
26	Raisin Bush				
25	Resurrection Plant				
19	Spike-thorn, Kraal				

Page No.	GRASSES/REEDS				
35	Blue Buffalo				
24	Bristle-leaved Red Top				
25	Common Russet				
34	Couch				
32	Feathered Chloris				
17	Fine Thatching				
29	Finger				
13	Golden Beard				
18	Guinea				
17	Gum				
12	Hairy Blue				
15	Narrow-leaved Turpentine				
33	Natal Red Top				
31	Reeds				
27	Silky Bushman				
28	Sorghum, Common Wild				
16	White Buffalo				
15	Wire				
16	Wool				

INSECTS

Page No.	INSECTS				
32	Ants				
32	Beetle, Dung				
36	Cricket, Common				
28	Dragonfly, Emperor				
27	Fly, Robber				
32	Millipede				
36	Moth, Death's Head Hawk				
36	Looper				
36	Praying Mantis				
21	Spider, Garbage Line				
18	Golden Brown Baboon				
21	Golden Orb Web				
18	Tropical Tent				
24	Wall Crab				
16	Termites, Snouted				
24	Tick, Hard				

REPTILES

Page No.	REPTILES				
32	Adder, Puff				
26	Agama, Southern rock				
29	Crocodile, Nile				
28	Frog, Foam nest				
28	Striped Stream				
21	Gecko, Tropical house				
26	Mamba, Black				
26	Monitor, Rock				
28	Water				
26	Python, African rock				
36	Skink, Common striped				
18	Snake, Spotted bush				
28	Terrapin, Cape				
20	Toad, Red				
32	Tortoise, Leopard				

Species Tick List

Tips for spotting

- The best times for game spotting are the early mornings and the late afternoons.
- Sit in a shady spot and wait patiently – like animals do.
- Listen and watch carefully.
- For best viewing drive at 20 km/h.

BIRDS

Page No.	BIRDS			
20	Babbler, Arrowmarked			
12	Pied			
20	Barbet, Blackcollared			
12	Crested			
23	Batis, Chinspot			
33	Bee-eater, Little			
33	Whitefronted			
22	Bulbul, Blackeyed			
32	Bunting, Goldenbreasted			
32	Rock			
34	Bustard, Kori			
27	Chat, Mocking			
30	Cormorant, Whitebreasted			
30	Dabchick			
30	Darter			
36	Dikkop, Spotted			
20	Dove, Cape Turtle			
20	Greenspotted			
20	Laughing			
22	Drongo, Forktailed			
30	Duck, Whitefaced			
31	Yellowbilled			
31	Eagle, African fish			
27	Black			
17	Blackbreasted snake			
34	Tawny			
34	Wahlberg's			
16	Egret, Cattle			
22	Firefinch, Jameson's			
22	Redbilled			
23	Flycatcher, Marico			

Page No.	BIRDS (continued)			
32	Francolin, Coqui			
32	Crested			
32	Natal			
32	Swainson's			
30	Goose, Egyptian			
30	Spurwinged			
20	Guineafowl, Helmeted			
30	Hamerkop			
31	Heron, Grey			
22	Hoopoe			
20	Hornbill, Redbilled			
20	Yellowbilled			
31	Ibis, Hadeda			
27	Kestrel, Rock			
23	Kingfisher, Brownhooded			
31	Pied			
23	Striped			
16	Kite, Blackshouldered			
34	Korhaan, Black			
34	Redcrested			
13	Lark, Rufousnaped			
13	Sabota			
23	Loerie, Grey			
27	Martin, Rock			
23	Mousebird, Speckled			
23	Whitebacked			
36	Nightjars			
22	Oriole, Blackheaded			
35	Ostrich			
36	Owl, Pearlspotted			
36	Spotted eagle			
20	Pigeon, Rock			
31	Plover, Threebanded			
20	Robin, Whitebrowed			
16	Roller, Lilacbreasted			
35	Secretarybird			
22	Shrike, Crimsonbreasted			
22	Fiscal			
20	Starling, Glossy			
27	Redwinged			
30	Swallow, Whitethroated			
34	Vulture, Cape			
34	Lappetfaced			
34	Whitebacked			
23	Waxbill, Blue			
31	Weaver, Lesser masked			
16	Whydah, Pintailed			
22	Woodhoopoe, Redbilled			
22	Woodpecker, Cardinal			

MAMMALS

Page No.	MAMMALS			
36	Aardvark			
37	Aardwolf			
13	Antelope, Sable			
24	Baboon, Chacma			
17	Buffalo			
37	Bushbaby, Lesser			
19	Bushbuck			
37	Caracal			
14	Cheetah			
36	Civet, African			
25	Dassie, Rock			
18	Duiker, Common			
12	Eland			
21	Elephant			
13	Gemsbok			
36	Genet, Large-spotted			
21	Giraffe			
37	Hare, Scrub			
34	Korhaan, Black			
14	Hartebeest, Red			
29	Hippopotamus			
37	Hyaena, Brown			
19	Impala			
14	Jackal, Black-backed			
24	Klipspringer			
12	Kudu			
25	Leopard			
15	Lion			
33	Ostrich			
36	Mongoose, Slender			
18	Monkey, Vervet			
36	Porcupine			
28	Reedbuck, Common			
12	Mountain			
19	Rhinoceros, Black			
15	White			
14	Springbok			
18	Squirrel, Tree			
18	Steenbok			
14	Tssessebe			
33	Warthog			
29	Waterbuck, Common			
15	Wildebeest, Blue			
13	Zebra, Burchell's			

Young cheetahs at play

INDEX

Aardvark 36
Aardwolf 37
Acacia karroo 16
Acacia mellifera 22, 52
Acacia tortilis 16
Adder, Puff 32
Acherontia atropos 36
Acinonyx jubatus 14
Aepyceros melampus 19
African Civet 36
African Rock Python 26
Agama atra 26
Agama, Southern Rock 26
Alcelaphus buselaphus 14
Aloe marlothii 13
Aloe, Mountain 13
Alopochen aegyptiacus 30
Anas undulata 31
Anax imperator 28
Andropogon chinensis 12
Anhinga melanogaster 30
Ant 32, 36
Antbear 36
Antelope, Sable 13
Anthephora pubescens 16
Antidorcas marsupialis 14
Aquila rapax 34
Aquila wahlbergi 34
Aquila verreauxii 27
Ardea cinerea 31
Ardeotis kori 34
Asilidae, Family 27

Babbler, Arrowmarked 20
  Pied 12
Baboon Spider, Golden Brown 18
Baboon, Chacma 25, 46
Baile Picnic Site 48, 56
Baile Plain 48, 57
Bakgatla 40, 44
Bakgatla Camp 49, 51
Bakgatla Gate 49
Bakubung 45
Bakubung Camp 48, 54
Bakubung Gate 49
Barbet, Blackcollared 20
  Crested 12
  Pied 12
Batis molitor 23
Batis, Chinspot 23
Batlhako 40
Bean, Sumach 28
Batlhako Tribe 40
Bee-eater, Little 33
  Whitefronted 33
Beech, Transvaal 23, 6, 53
Beetle, Dung 32, 37
Belambra tree 56
Bidens pilosa 32, 57
Bitis arietans arietans 32
Black-jack 32
Black Mamba 26
Black Rhinoceros 19, 15, 26, 30, 42
Black Thorn 22, 52
Black-backed Jackal 14
Blue Buffalo Grass 35
Blue Grass, Hairy 12
Blue Wildebeest 15, 7
Boer War 41
Bogwera 41
Bomamauwane 36
Boscia foetida 21, 50
Bostrychia hagedash 31
Bristle-leaved Red Top 24
Brown Hyaena 37, 54
Bubo africanus 36
Bubulcus ibis 16
Bucerotidae, Family 20
Buffalo 17, 31, 45, 55
Buffalo Grass, Blue 35
  White 16
Buffalo-thorn 19, 47, 55
Bufo carens 20
Bulbul, Blackeyed 22

Bunting, Goldenbreasted 32
  Rock 32
Burchell's Zebra 13
Burhinus capensis 36
Bush Snake, Spotted 18
Bushbaby, Lesser 37
Bushbuck 19
Bushmen/San 39
Bushwillow, Large-fruited 12
  Red 12, 7
  River 28
  Velvet 12
Bustard, Kori 34, 16

Cabbage Tree 24, 6
Camps
  Bakgatla 49
  Bakubung 48
  Kololo 48
  Kwa Maritane 49
  Mankwe 49
  Manyane 49
  Metswedi 48
  Tshukudu 48
Canis mesomelas 14
Cape Terrapin 28
Caprimulgidae, Family 36
Caracal 37
Carissa bispinosa 20
Cenchrus ciliaris 35
Ceratotherium simum 15
Cercopithecus aethiops 18
Ceryle rudis 31
Chacma Baboon 25
Charadrius tricollaris 31
Chat, Mocking 27
Cheetah 14
Chiromantis xerampelina 28
Chloris virgata 32
Chloris, Feathered 32
Chrysopogon serrulatus 13
Church Site 48, 57
Circaetus gallicus/pectoralis 17
Civet, African 36
Civettictis civetta 36
Colius colius 23
Colius striatus 23
Columba guinea 20
Columbidae, Family 20
Combretum apiculatum 12
Combretum erythrophyllum 28
Combretum imberbe 14
Combretum molle 12
Combretum zeyheri 12
Common Cricket 36
Common Duiker 18
Common Reedbuck 28, 56
Common Russet Grass 25
Common Striped Skink 36
Common Tree Euphorbia 24, 53
Common Waterbuck 29
Common Wild Pear 26
Common Wild Sorghum 28
Connochaetes taurinus 15
Coracias caudata 16
Cormorant, Whitebreasted 30
Corythaixoides concolor 23
Couch Grass 34
Cricket, Common 36
Crocodile, Nile 29, 11
Crocodylus niloticus 29
Croton gratissimus 26
Cussonia species 24
Cyclosa species 21
Cymbopogon plurinodis 15
Cynodon dactylon 34
Cyrtophora species 18

Dabchick 30
Damaliscus lunatus 14
Darter 30
Dassie, Rock 25
Death's Head Hawk Moth 36
Dendroaspis polylepis 26
Dendrocygna viduata 30
Dendropicos fuscescens 22
Diceros bicornis 19
Dicrurus adsimilis 22
Digitaria erianttha 29
Dikgofa 24
Dikkop, Spotted 36
Dikorwe 20

Ditshoswane 32
Dombeya rotundifolia 26
Doratogonus annulipes 32
Dove, Cape Turtle 20
  Greenspotted 20
  Laughing 20
Dragonfly, Emperor 28
Driefontein 48, 56
Drongo, Forktailed 22
Duck, Whitefaced 30
  Yellowbilled 31
Duiker, Common 18
Dung Beetle 32, 57
Dyke 3

Eagle, African Fish 31, 52
  Black 27, 52
  Blackbreasted Snake 17
  Martial 18
  Tawny 34
  Wahlberg's 34
Earthquake 2, 3
Egret, Cattle 16
Ehretia rigida 22
Eland 12, 19, 56
Elanus caeruleus 16
Elephant 21, 17, 28, 31, 42, 45
Elephantorrhiza burkei 28
Elionurus muticus 15
Emberiza flaviventris 32
Emberiza tahapisi 32
Emperor Dragonfly 28
Equus burchellii 13
Eragrostis gummiflua 17
Erosion 43, 4, 6, 8
Erythropygia leucophrys 20
Estrildidae, Family 22
Euphorbia ingens 24, 54
Euphorbia, Common Tree
  24, 53 41
Eupodotis afra 34
Eupodotis ruficrista 34
European settlers 41

Falco tinnunculus 27
Faurea saligna 23, 53
Feathered Chloris 32
Felis caracal 37
Fern, Hard 26
Fever-berry, Lavender 26
Ficus soldanella 24
Fig, Large-leaved Rock 24
Fine Thatching Grass 17
Finger Grass 29
Firefinch, Jameson's 22
  Redbilled 22
Fish Eagle Picnic Site 49, 53
Flattie, Wall Crab Spider 24
Flourite Mine 49, 54
Fly, Robber 27
Flycatcher, Marico 23
Foam Nest Frog 28, 31
Formicidae, Family 32
Foyaite 2-4, 10, 53, 54, 56, 57
Francolin, Coqui 32
  Crested 32
  Natal 32
  Swainson's 32
Francolinus coqui 32
Francolinus natalensis 32
Francolinus sephaena 32
Francolinus swainsonii 32
Fringillidae, Family 32
Frog, Foam Nest 28
  Striped Stream 28

Galago moholi 37
Galerella sanguinea 33
Garbage Line Spider 21
Gates
  Bakgatla 49
  Bakubung 49
  Kwa Maritane 49
  Manyane 49
Geographic Centre 49, 55
Gecko, Tropical House 21
Gemsbok 13, 56
Genet, Large-spotted 36, 37
Geological sites 5
Genetta tigrina 36
Geochelone pardalis babcocki 32
Giraffa camelopardalis 21
Giraffe 21, 15, 28
Glaucidium perlatum 36
Golden Beard Grass 13
Golden Brown Baboon Spider 18
Golden Orb Web Spider 21
Goose, Egyptian 30
  Spurwinged 30
Gopane 26, 28, 46